C0-BWY-683

REFRIGERATOR PRAYERS
FOR
ORDINARY PEOPLE

BY
BETH LINDSAY TEMPLETON

Conversations with God
About the Details of Life

Refrigerator Prayers for Ordinary People

Conversations with God About the Details of Life

By Beth Lindsay Templeton

Copyright © Beth Lindsay Templeton, 2014

Contact Beth: **beth@oewo.org**

www.oureyeswereopened.org

www.bltempleton.com

www.noonatnightpublications.com

All rights reserved. No part of this book may be used or reproduced by any means, graphic, electronic, or mechanical, including photocopying, recording, taping or by any information storage retrieval system without the written permission of the publisher except in the case of brief quotations embodied in critical articles and reviews. New Revised Standard Version of the Bible, copyright 1989 by the Division of Christian Education of the National Council of Churches in the United States of America. Used by permission. All Rights Reserved.

Because of the dynamic nature of the Internet, any Web addresses or links contained in this book may have changed since publication and may no longer be valid.

The views expressed in this work are solely those of the author and do not necessarily reflect the views of the publisher, and the publisher hereby disclaims any responsibility for them.

Printed in the United States of America

For Dorcas and Denton Lindsay

"Rejoice always,
pray without ceasing,
give thanks in all circumstances;
for this is the will of God in Christ Jesus for you.
Do not quench the Spirit."

I Thessalonians 5:16-19

Acknowledgements

This book developed over a long period. For years I wrote prayers that appeared infrequently in the newsletter of United Ministries in Greenville, SC. People told me they posted these prayers on their refrigerators. The supporters of United Ministries affirmed the process that eventually became this book. Thanks to each of you who let me know that you posted something I wrote on your refrigerator.

One of my early memories is my mom's transcribing the taped prayers that our minister, Dr. C.Newman Faulconer, used in worship services and at other occasions. She demonstrated early to me the value of written prayers. Thanks, Mama.

To all those authors who developed prayers to be used in Sunday liturgies, thank you. Your varied styles enriched me and the worship services I have led in ways that I do not even know. I depended on the calls to worship, prayers of dedication, intercessory prayers, and benedictions you wrote. Your gifts of words and creative phrases inspired me.

Thanks to the developers of Facebook because this is where I first published some of these prayers. I discovered a way to share my own prayers thereby addressing the prayer needs of ordinary people.

Thanks to Rob Krabbe who encouraged me to keep writing without worrying about how to get a book into print. Without his knowledge, this material may have slept in my computer for a long, long time.

Thanks to my husband, Jim, who takes wonderful care of me so that I have the time, freedom, and energy to do what I love to do! There's more I could say but he knows my heart.

Blessings,
Beth Lindsay Templeton
August, 2014

Introduction

Prayer is sacred. It is conversation with the Holy One, our God. Some printed prayers mean so much to us at a particular time in our lives that we make copies or rip them out of printed material and stick them on our refrigerator. They bear testimony that God is working in our lives.

For some people, prayer is real only when words such as Thee, Thou, and Thy are used. Others always use the same name for God in their prayers: Holy God, Father, Lord, Dear Jesus. Prayers come from overwhelming joy. Other prayers come from agony and suffering that is deep inside when we're facing loss, fear, or pain.

Some people seem to know how to pray aloud beautifully and spontaneously. Their words come from special places in the moment. The feelings that undergird such unplanned prayer touch something deep inside the listener. Other inspirational prayers are written. They grow out of meditation, thoughtful Bible reading, or deep study.

There are books about praying and books full of rich and meaningful prayers. All of these resources can be helpful for the faith journey.

But sometimes we just want to chat with God. Tevye in the musical *Fiddler on the Roof* talks with the Lord God Almighty as if God is standing right there. Those prayers are real. Whatever is on Tevye's mind is worthy of talking with God about...right then! His prayers are gutsy, they are quirky, and if refrigerators existed, they might end up on one!

It is in this spirit that many of the prayers in this book were written. God is both near and far. God is as close as our breath and as far as the stars or even beyond. God's relationship with us invites honest dialogue. Form and vocabulary are not as important as being real, owning the positives and negatives of our human condition, and yearning for a deep connection with our triune God.

In using this resource, you will note a couple of things.

1. The one God has lots of names in these prayers. The Hebrew name most commonly used for God was Yahweh, often translated as "I am who I am" or "I will be who I will be." The name Yahweh allows for humans to experience God in a variety of ways. These different ways of encountering God encourage using different ways to address God. How we understand our relation to God and God's relationship with us often depends on what is going on in our lives at the time. Therefore, we might call out to God in different ways: Holy One, God of the Silent Spaces, Mighty God, Lord Jesus, and many others.

2. Some prayers refer to specific people by name. Even though the names may have been changed, the people are real. They had come to United Ministries, a faith-based organization in Greenville, SC, that provides life changing opportunities to people. While they waited in the lobby to talk with personnel, a very compassionate volunteer, Susan, asked each one to tell her about the most important thing he or she had learned. Their wisdom is captured in some of the prayers.

There is space under each printed prayer for you to make notes, jot down a word or two, or even doodle or sketch. I encourage you to use this space for whatever comes to your mind or spirit.

May you find in these prayers whatever God wants to give you and whatever you are seeking in your journey of faith. May they resonate in the deep places of your heart, mind, and soul.

January 1

God of Endings and Beginnings, we've rung in another new year. We want the slate to be wiped clean. Why do we think we must have a date on the calendar to begin anew? Why can't we lean on you for our sense of renewal, refreshment, and recommitment to things that matter?

God of life, be with us as we strive to be the people you are leading us to be. Expand us so we can be open to the magnificent and release the mediocre. Instill…

> Vision in our hearts;
>
> Insight in our minds;
>
> Compassion in our ears;
>
> Delight in our eyes;
>
> Dedication in our hands.

It's a new year.

Thank you for yet another opportunity to get it right! Amen

January 2

Companion of the Brave, Mighty God, I praise you that you are who you are...even though I really cannot fathom even a speck of that. Help me be brave in this new year of life. All I know is that you are love; you keep your promises; you give grace; and you come to me as creator, redeemer, sustainer, father, mother, Jesus, Christ, and Holy Spirit. May you always abide in me and I in you. This is what I ask on this second day of the new year. Amen

January 3

Ho hum. Holy God. That's how I feel. Ho hum. The holidays are over. The dark of winter is here. Ho hum. I hope it is okay that I don't feel very worshipful or full of praise right now. Ho hum. Hang in there with me until the doldrums pass. I know you are here. It's just…well…ho hum. Amen

January 4

Thank you for people who share their wisdom with me. Others might look at them and believe they have nothing noteworthy to share about life because of their clothing, hair, teeth, or smell. But they don't know Kyle who said, "Think before you act! All actions have consequences." Or Martha who said, "Try to live a stress free life by turning it over to God and stop seeking everybody's approval." They've never heard Ed say that he needed to learn passion and purpose or Samantha say, "Don't give up when things get hard." Thank you for these wise people who share life lessons so freely. Keep them close to your love and grace. Amen

January 5

God of Delight, thank you for the many wonders that you surround us with. We get in our ruts and then...then...you shine a light on someone or something that tickles our fancy. You surprise us out of our usual ways of thinking. You tease us into a new interest. You invite us into amazement at something we've always known was there but never really saw. You offer us life!

Thank you for shaking us up. Help us to embrace your delight so we may share it with others. Amen

January 6

God of Epiphany, today is the day the Christian Church celebrates the visit of the Wise Men to the Christ Child thereby expanding the good news to the gentiles. It also celebrates the baptism of Jesus. Epiphany is also a sudden, intuitive perception or insight into the reality or essential meaning of something, often sparked by some simple, ordinary occurrence or experience.

Holy God of Unique Perceptions, keep us aware in our everyday worlds of the glimpses of you and your activity among us. Let us not become complacent of your interventions in our lives and our communities. Help us always to see coincidences as your choosing to work anonymously. Amen

January 7

God of Hope, forgive us for not being amazed.

You surround us with love and we do not notice.

You undergird us with strength and we do not acknowledge this power.

You cherish us with grace and we say "whatever."

You discipline us with compassion and we complain.

You entice us with hope and we sigh dejectedly.

Forgive us for not noticing.

Forgive us for taking your gifts to us for granted.

Forgive us for being bland.

We want to be who you lead us to be. Help us to quit dragging our feet. Amen

January 8

Everlasting God, she said, "No one ever made me feel that special or important before. That made all the difference." How this statement must break your heart. We do not reach out to others to let them know how important they are. Instead we judge, look down upon, demean, ignore, discount, and blame. Forgive us for not reflecting your love and grace. Fill us so we can see those who need to feel special or important. Help us know what they need to nourish their spirit and then make us the instruments of your care. Amen

January 9

God of Healing Energy, sometimes I'm just tired. I really don't want to have to care about anyone else. I want to be left alone to wallow in my own fatigue or apathy. Is it possible for you to stand close but just to leave me alone for a bit? I really could use a hole to crawl into…only for a moment. We'll chat later. Amen

January 10

Mighty Redeemer, save me from myself. I think I know exactly what I should be doing, how I should be doing it, and what the results will be. Forgive my hubris. Turn me upside down so I will finally see life as you want me to see it. Lead me in the ways you want me to go because only there will I find the fulfillment and joy I seek. I depend on your love and grace, Most Loving Savior. Amen

January 11

Maker of All Things, he screamed, "This is public property. You can't make me leave." Why did this taunt get my blood going? Why did I assert that this property was indeed private and that I could do anything I wanted...even put him on trespass notice? Of course, I wanted to protect others who are on this property. I even wanted to protect our property. But why did I have to become so adamant that this was mine to decide about?

You are the giver of all we enjoy. Without you none of our successes could have happened. We want to honor you and also protect other people and other things. We are divided about what is the loving and faithful thing to do. If we need forgiveness, please grant us your pardon. If it is wisdom for such situations that we lack, then we ask for your guidance. Help us never to assume that our decisions are always pure even though they may be prudent. Keep us mindful of those who, for whatever reason, need to assert their right to be. Amen

January 12

You have told us, Lover of Our Souls, what you require of us: to do justice, love mercy, and to walk humbly with you. We know what to do. We just don't often have the will to do it. We want retribution rather than justice, closed hearts rather than mercy, and walking in our own power and pride rather than with you. Forgive us and lead us to claim your will for us. Fill us with desire to be the kind of people you have created us to be. Let us overflow with faith and may our actions reflect that intense commitment of relationship with you. Amen

—From

Micah 6:6-8

January 13

Eternal God, I want to understand. An old native American proverb says, "Tell me and I'll forget. Show me, and I may not remember. Involve me, and I'll understand." Involve me. So often I want to be a bystander. I want to...

Watch rather than step into the circle.

Look *around* rather than *into* the situation.

Ignore rather than put my hands in.

Pretend rather than acknowledge.

Close my eyes rather than see.

Creator of my world, help me understand. Amen

January 14

Today, Triune God, let the words adapted from a reflection on Matthew 25, written by John Stott years ago, settle into my heart and take root there.

"I was hungry and you formed a humanities club to discuss my hunger. Thank you.

I was imprisoned and you crept off quietly to your chapel to pray for my releases. Nice.

I was naked and in your mind you debated the morality of my appearance. What good did that do?

I was sick and you knelt and thanked God for your health. But I needed you.

I was homeless and you preached to me of the shelter of the love of God. I wish you'd taken me home.

I was lonely and you left me alone to pray for me. Why didn't you stay?

You seem so holy, so close to God; but I'm still very hungry, lonely, cold, and still in pain. Does it matter?" Amen

—From

www.eatfeedlovelive.com/2013/10/i-was-hungry-and-you-formed-humanities.html, web search 8.2.14

January 15

Holy God, you know we love heroes. We collect action figures, we cheer at movies when the bad guy gets stomped, and we read about and watch athletes. Help us to learn and try to imitate real heroes ... people like Martin Luther King, Jr. ...whose birthday is today.

Rev. King was a man who believed that fighting and meanness were not the ways to win. Winning meant loving and speaking the truth.

He was a man who was not afraid to do what was right, even when he might get hurt. Doing right meant being brave and courageous.

He was a man who taught others how to be heroes by reaching out to people who were hungry and needed help. Being strong meant helping people who were weak.

Oh, my God, help us to be real heroes with our friends and family. Help us to win ... by loving and telling the truth. Help us to do right ...by being brave and courageous. Help us to be strong ... by reaching out to others who are weak.

We trust in you and lean on your strength to strengthen us. Go with us this day.

With confidence in your love, we pray. Amen

January 16

God of Justice, yesterday was the actual birthday of the Rev. Dr. Martin Luther King, Jr. He once said, "Most people…are thermometers that record or register the temperature of majority opinion, not thermostats that transform and regulate the temperature of society." Help me be a thermostat. Amen

—From

http://www.thirdworldtraveler.com/Martin%20Luther %20King/MLKing_quotes.html, web search 11.18.12

January 17

God of All Good Gifts, thank you for all the many ways you enrich my life.

For electricity that lights my home;

For natural gas that keeps me warm;

For phones and computers that allow me to keep in touch with friends and family;

For running water that nourishes and cleans;

For tubs that offer soothing soaks after long days;

I know that many in our community do not enjoy these same wonders. Let me never take them for granted. Amen.

January 18

God of All Love, hugs are important. Thanks to Miroslav Volf's book, *Exclusion and Embrace*, I realized the many decisions about hugs. You have to decide how committed you are to the hug. Shall you do a side to side hug, an air hug, or one of those that involve full body contact—you know—when you've really been hugged. And then you have to decide whether you will initiate the hug or hang back so the other person takes the lead. How long shall you embrace? But the most important part of the hug is when you release the other. You've shown the depth of your feelings for the other and now you allow the person to go about living in his or her own special and particular way. Holy One, help me to offer hugs that enrich and not smother another. Help me to know when to initiate and when to release. Only then can the other know how deeply I care. Amen

—From

Miroslav Volf, Exclusion and Embrace, A Theological Exploration of Identity, Otherness, and Reconciliation, Abingdon Press: Nashville, TN, 1996

January 19

Proclaimer of Justice, justice is seeing where the scales of life are not balanced for another and then bringing balance. Is it really that easy...and that hard? Help me live into the deep and profound truths of that insight. Inspire me to be a person whose passion is justice...in word and in deed. Amen

January 20

Okay, God. What's going on? Where are you? You promise that you love the world and want only its good health and beauty. So...what's happening? Where is the evidence of your love and vision? Why is nothing changing? Who is in charge here? Who's supposed to be helping the world and everything that lives and moves in it? What are we to be looking for? How are we supposed to be faithful? Why can't you just zap everything and let us off the hook?

That's not the way you are. We are to be partners with you. You have shown us the way. Okay. Amen

January 21

God of Righteousness,

Why does whining feel so good when we do it and yet, is so aggravating when someone else does it?

Why do we have great excuses for shirking our duty and yet, we think others are lazy when they do it?

Why do we make only "simple, human" mistakes, and yet others are careless and stupid when they do the same thing?

Why do we believe we are self-made people and forget all those who helped us get here?

Help us relinquish our focus on ourselves alone and learn to feel life as the other person might. Amen

January 22

Hey, God, sometimes life is just plain scary. The news, dire predictions made by all kinds of people, office gossip, fears claimed by family members, not to mention television shows, all reinforce bottom line anxieties. Let me rest in you. Help me hold to the promises that nothing can separate me from you. Sustain me by your quiet grace. Undergird me with your wisdom. And when I get too nutsy with fear, bring me calming people, books, music, and visions that help me reconnect to the reality that you are God and you love me and the entire world. In you there is nothing to fear. I need have no overwhelming anxiety when I pull away from the source of my terror and push toward your love. Thank you. Amen

January 23

Holy God of Beauty, today is a good hair day. Thank you for creating me in such a way that being happy with my hair today makes a big difference in how I approach everyone and everything. To some people this might seem trivial but you've designed us so that even trivial things are wonderful gifts and remind us of the beauty of your creation and of being alive. Praise you from whom all blessings flow…even good hair days! Amen

January 24

God of All Times and Places, remind me that you are here and there. Because I can't be with my friend who is hurting so much, I need you to be there. I need you to be here with me because I ache for the pain my friend is experiencing. I also depend on knowing that you were with me in the past with all its good and bad, that you are here today, in the present, and that you will be with me in the future, no matter what comes. You will be with me in the celebrations, in the ordinariness of life, and in the challenges. What a wondrous God you are. You are as close as my own breath and as vast as the universe and beyond. Your awesomeness is overwhelming. Thank you for being in all times and places. Amen

January 25

God of Wonder, my screensaver has a picture of Stonehenge. Having stood by those magnificent stones and felt tiny, I realize that sometimes we are more in awe of something as grand as the stone circle than we are of you. You who make the hawk soar, you who put the mane on the horse, you who make rain, snow, and dew, you who shut in the sea with doors, you are more than we can ever imagine...and yet, somehow, we want to take you for granted. We box you in. We see you as a pebble rather than as larger than life itself.

Help us to experience the awe that you so rightly deserve. Lead us out of our limitations and into the wondrous reality of your holy being. Amen

January 26

Holy God Who Cannot Be Contained In Our Words, we are limited in how we see and experience you. However, we can see evidence of your presence everywhere. When we look at ordinary items, we can be reminded of your love and grace in our lives. When we see a hairbrush, we remember that you count the hairs on our heads, that you know us that intimately. When we work at a computer, we know that you juggle many more bits of information within the universe daily. When we taste a cool glass of iced tea, we remember that you are indeed living water in our lives.

Help us to be always aware of your presence surrounding us every day. Amen

January 27

God of the Word, our world is filled with words, words, words. Are we really communicating? Help us hear your word amidst all the clanking. Give us ears to listen and hearts to heed. Amen

January 28

God of Love, sometimes I just don't care. I don't want to be bothered by the world. I don't want to reach out and share your love. I don't even want to try to love myself. I pray that you have patience with me when I'm in that place. Love me back to wanting to be engaged again. Amen

January 29

Holy God, I pray for gang leaders and drug dealers. They obviously have wonderful talents for leadership and entrepreneurial ventures. I grieve that they have no place to use those gifts except in ways that hurt rather than help others. Speak to *their* minds so they can soften their hearts to accept good rather than evil in their lives. Speak to *our* minds so we can discover ways to guide them to channel the wonderful skills that are so evident. Chasten us to see the creative rather than the destructive. Convict us to reach out for health rather than harm. Help us to see opportunity rather than wring our hands in despair and helplessness. Help us to love as you love. We cannot reach out with love nor do we even want to do it without your prodding. Support all of us, including the gang leaders and drug dealers. Amen

January 30

God of all Reality, what's with this reality television? Have we moved so far from you that we think the garbage we watch is somehow connected to the reality that is you? Your reality is vaster than the biggest thing we can imagine. Your reality, rolled into one stupendous gorgeousness, is more beautiful than all the beauty we've experienced. Your reality is more loving than the most love we have ever felt multiplied by a zillion. Why do we gorge on reality that is not? Encourage us to feed ourselves with reality that soothes our souls, nourishes our spirits, and supports our growth in your truth and grace. Amen

January 31

Healing God, she shared her fear with me. All I could do was listen to her and for your guidance. Thanks for being with us in this sacred moment. Amen

February 1

God of My Present, I'm confused. I want to know what's going to happen...next week, next month, next year. Since you're not filling in any details, I'm doing that for you. I'm imagining what the future holds for me, for people I love, for the community in which I work, and for the world that surrounds me. But, unfortunately, when I do that, I never get it right. Whatever "it" is that I'm envisioning, "it" never happens the way I thought. Occasionally I get close, but never exact. Is that what it means, then, to trust in you? To rest in you? To live in the present that you give to me? To trust that the future for me and everyone else is in your hands?

I guess that what I'm to do is to work in the present with hope for the future, accepting that the outcomes are hidden in your love. Please keep me grounded in the present so that I can rejoice in you, whatever the future holds. Amen

February 2

Holy God, do you sometimes think that we humans are just silly? Groundhog Day? Predicting the weather and change of seasons by a furry rodent that may or may not see its shadow? Maybe if we could see a bit of our living from your viewpoint, we'd see how we take some things much too seriously and totally ignore things that truly matter. Help us focus on only the really important things and ignore the shallow. Then help us to know which is which. Amen

February 3

God of Joy, thank you for the gift of laughter. For a truly transcendent activity, nothing can beat tears-in-your-eyes hee-hawing. When I throw my head back and laugh out loud, I forget myself; I forget whatever is going on in my life; and I forget others around me. When I laugh, I connect with all that is good in you and the world you have given. The act of laughing with a deep sense of delight and abandonment lets me fly on wings as eagles. Thank you, Most Loving God. Amen

February 4

God of Change, thank you that someone coined the words, "This too shall pass." What a gift for living life with gratitude, humility, and hope. When something bad happens, we know "this too shall pass." When something wonderful happens and we want to stay in that euphoria, we know "this too shall pass." When we fear, "this too shall pass." When we celebrate, "this too shall pass." The ebbs and flows of life are captured in the beautiful words, "this too shall pass." Help us to always remember that whatever happens, all life is in your loving care and *this* shall never pass! Praise you, Alleluia! Amen

February 5

God of Comfort, friends are living with grief and fear. Be with them. Surround them with people who show compassion by holding their hands, sitting in silence with them, providing a simple meal, and offering other gentle kindnesses so they will know they are loved and cared for. Fill the hands of caregivers with grace, wisdom, and skill. As they live through this dark time, give them hope for what's on the other side of this journey for each of them. Help all of us to be the answer to this prayer we make. Amen

February 6

Hallelujah, Hallelujah! I'm shouting out praises for no particular reason. It just seems like a good thing to do today. Sing with joy, dance with abandon, laugh with exuberance. Hallelujah! I'm alive and you are God! Hosanna in the highest. Amen

February 7

God of Health, thank you for the person who invented aspirin. Aspirin can help our hearts, make headaches go away, bring down fevers and reduce inflammation. However, like so many of your good gifts, it can also harm us when we use too much. But for all its good effects, thank you. You are more than the God of the universe. You are also the God of the itty bitty details. How wonderful is that? Help us remember to use your gifts as you intend. So thanks for the person who invented aspirin. Amen

February 8

Holy God, our world seems full of grief. In countries hit by natural disaster, people struggle with losses of all kinds. Other people continue to lose jobs or to get turned down for employment. People grieve over death, illness, and disappointment. War torn countries all over the globe are filled with people who are overwhelmed with loss of security, faith, life, and property. At such times, we wonder where you are. And then we realize that you are here, in the midst of such crucifying times. Help us to do what we can to alleviate grief and to comfort the mourner while we wait patiently for the resurrection. Amen

February 9

God of Great Conversions, I confess that I may not be evolved enough so that I can give everything. I pray that you help me become mindful of my automatic spending and time habits. Maybe then I'll become more aware of all the things I hold back from you, the world, and the people you so love. Open up my heart to share more of those untouched gifts. Amen

February 10

God of Choice, sometimes something comes our way that flatters our innermost being. Someone gives us the opportunity to be bigger, more important, or more powerful. And yet, how do we know this is a gift from you? You have given us choice but not always laced that option with clarity. Is that part of listening more closely to you? To leaning more on you? If this is of you, make it stronger. If not, let it weaken and lose its fascination. Amen

February 11

God of the Unknown, what happens when people ignore you? They make you small, they domesticate you, they disempower you, or they reject you. How do you, holy God, tolerate such behavior from us? How do you love us even when we act so stupidly? We've got some lessons to learn yet, don't we? Please gently open us up to awe and wonder. Help us look wide-eyed rather than continue our practice of keeping our eyes low and unfocused. Course your life-giving energy and love through us. Enliven us with your grace. And please, be patient with us through all this. Amen

February 12

God of Wisdom, Rabindranath Tagore said, "I slept and dreamt that life was joy. I awoke and saw that life was service. I acted and behold, service was joy." May this be part of my life. Amen

—From

http://www.brainyquote.com/quotes/quotes/r/rabindr ana134933.html Web search 10.16.12

February 13

Loving Jesus Who Called the Little Ones to You, I pray for all children...

For those who are dearly loved by their parents;

For those who are seen only as a burden;

For those who eat healthy, nutritious meals;

For those, who, when they eat, eat whatever they can find;

For those who know that they will succeed at whatever they attempt;

For those who are told daily that they are failures;

For those who rarely experience the death of people they love;

For those who know too many people who have died untimely deaths;

Open our hearts to all children. Cause us unrest until we find ways to love children in the ways they deserve as your beloved little ones. Amen

February 14

God of Love, today is the day for lovers. May couples find pleasure in being together and sharing tokens of affection. For those without a person to love deeply and to be loved by, bring someone into their day who shares with them that they are important and special. When you want me to be someone who reaches out to that lonely person, give me the words, show me the actions, and lead me to see this one through your eyes. Everyone deserves to be loved and to feel special. Holy God, find lots of partners today to share your amazing love and grace in this hurting world. Amen

February 15

Most Holy God, today I saw a homeless man break off part of his sandwich to feed the pigeons. He, who has so little, took care of your creatures. Help me to be so generous and caring. Amen

February 16

God, Giver of Beauty, thank you for color. I love purple and you've given so many shades of it...lavender, amethyst, periwinkle, wine, royal, plum, and so many more. If I can love the huge variety of purple in our world, why is it that skin color becomes such a problem for so many of us? Amen

February 17

God of Relationships, help us be more thoughtful during these winter days about whose we are and how we demonstrate that connection to others. Amen

February 18

Loving God, you have made us and love us in all our many ways of being. You love us no matter what we do—good or bad. You love us when we live big and when we live small. You love us when we make you proud and when we greatly disappoint you. Thank you for that love. Inspire us to strive to be the kinds of people who are easy for you to love. Help us be grateful for those times of chastisement when you need to get our attention. And please, God, help us to learn quickly!!! Amen

February 19

God of Healing, I pray for those people who are sick and whose illness is made worse, if not terminal, because they are worried about how they will pay for the services they need. They worry that their family will be overburdened by their medical costs. They worry they will receive inadequate or secondary care because they do not have the resources that others in our community have. Give us the courage to do what is necessary to ensure that all in our community can receive the care they need in loving, compassionate ways. Keep reminding us that all of us are your dearly beloved children. We are family. Amen

February 20

God of Mystery, John L. Bell, compiled a group of songs that he called *There Is One Among Us.*

Who is that One?

Is it you, Lord Jesus, who moves among us and we are not aware?

Is it a person who is in pain that no one notices?

Is it a wise one who can share with us what we are searching for?

Is it a lonely person who despairs of anyone ever noticing her?

Is it a joy-filled person who can delight our spirit?

Is it a grieving person who has just had a dream to explode?

Of course, it IS you among us. You move among us in pain, with wisdom, in loneliness, with joy, and in grief. Help us search for you and find you...as one among us. Amen

—*From*

John L. Bell, There Is One Among Us, GIA Publications, Inc.: Chicago, IL, 1999

February 21

Hm-m-m-m God, what shall I have for lunch today? Shall I eat quiche, soup, a meat-and-three, a sandwich, a salad, or a hamburger? What a choice. How shall I decide? What shall it be?

Oh, my God, forgive me! I'm concerned about what I shall eat and never considered those who have absolutely nothing or will eat whatever the soup kitchen is serving today. How can you stand it when we are so focused on our little selves and fail to look at all the people in our community and our world who need so much more than the insignificant things we agonize over? Thank you for loving us even when we are so small-minded. Keep loving us into more open and generous hearts. Keep holding us as you convert our spirits for compassion and service. Amen

February 22

Awesome God, you've given us the gift of choice. Sometimes, however, that gift feels more like a curse than a blessing. Scott Peck once said, "[T]o exercise power is to make decisions, and the process of making decisions with total awareness is often infinitely more painful than making decisions with limited or blunted awareness." Be with us in those times of painful decisions. Help us to feel your presence undergirding us and guiding us through those times of unknown and "what-ifs." Amen

—From

Scott Peck, The Road Less Traveled, A New Psychology of Love, Traditional Values and Spiritual Growth, Simon and Schuster: New York , NY, 1978, p 75.

February 23

God of Surprises, thank you for the delight of unexpected pleasures: biting into a luscious clementine orange, the e-mail comment that makes us laugh out loud, the phone call from someone from the past, and the light glistening through the clouds. Help us always to be mindful of the gifts that brighten our lives and remind us of your constant love for us. May we be that gift to others. Amen

February 24

God of the Loving Heart, when people say things that baffle us, when they try to hurt us with words ("all for our own good"), or when they malign us, help us move beyond our anger, confusion, and dismay to a place of dispassion. Keep us from letting their words close down our loving spirit. Lead us to let go of whatever hurt seeps into our being. Support us so we can hold them to you with compassion. Amen

February 25

Our Creator and Our Teacher, teach us to live each day as if it were the last one we had. Push us to enjoy life fully, to nourish relationships with others, and to complete our mission for the day. When we go to bed at night, fill us with gratitude to you for a day well lived. Amen

February 26

Inspiring God, thank you for the words of writers who say what we wanted to say but could not. Thank you for the notes of musicians who help us soar as we wanted but could not. Thank you for the colors of painters who help us see what is true but we could not. For these many gifts, thank you. Amen

—From

http:www/parpdoxicalcommandments.com

web search 10.16.12

February 27

God of Time and Place, why in the world did you allow someone to create calendars? Now that we have them, we fill them with activities, meetings, appointments, projects, things to do, people to see, lists, messages to return, and on and on. We use them to be productive, efficient, important, and to prove our worthiness. The busier we are the more important we are. And now, we have instant messaging, communications, and connections 24-7. Why did you allow all this to happen?

Oh, (long pause), oh, (even longer pause), oh, (a really long pause). You created Sabbath for a reason. You put us in charge of our calendars and our 24-7 contacts. But you…you…even you…rested once a week. And I mean really rested. Help us to put appropriate boundaries and limitations on our calendars and all the rest.

Ah, there's that word again…rest. I'll take a deep breath. Holy Spirit, please, please breathe into me and unplug me. Help me fall in love with white space in my calendar! Amen

February 28

God of Holy Insights, thank you for Carl who said that listening is more important than talking. He said that his mother taught, "You'll never grow old when you look at the world through a child's eyes." Thank you for Carl and his words of wisdom. May they seep deep into my soul. Amen

March 1

God of Celebration, today I thank you for older people who exhibit joy in the life you have given them and who demonstrate how important laughter is. You richly bless all who know these delightful saints. Thank you for the gift of joy. Amen

March 2

Eternal Source of Peace, we sure could use some peace right now. People are being killed here and around the globe. People are dying due to poverty and unbelievable physical conditions. Anger and hatred fuel fear everywhere. Greed causes pain and violence. We really want peace but we don't want to work for it. Is there anything you can do about bringing in peace so we don't have to change our attitudes, priorities, beliefs, or our prejudices? No? Well, I guess that task just fell back into our laps. At least will you help us and prod us to change what we need to so we can participate in actually making peace? Thanks. Amen

March 3

God of All Compassion, how can we know what we need to do and still not do it? We know that:

Substandard housing negatively affects health.

Long-term stress can lead to pre-term births and low birth weight.

Four-year-old kindergartens improve graduation rates and reduce incarceration rates.

Plastics pollute our waters and kill our wildlife.

That's mentioning only a few of the things we know. How is it we know this and still do nothing about it? Please help us to wake up, be responsible, and make difficult decisions. Strengthen us, enrage us, and guide us to help make your world what you intend it to be for all your children. Amen

March 4

Mighty God, we praise you for who you are in our lives and our world. Even when we are not aware of your presence, we know you are here. When we wonder what the future holds, we can be confident that whatever it is, you are there. When we are alone, we know that even then, you are holding us up. We are humbled by your being with us and astounded that you care so much. Thank you for being more than we deserve and for loving us, no matter what. Amen

March 5

Shelter from the Storm, we lift up to you those who are being battered by the storms of life. Whether the storm is hitting them in their physical life, their emotional life, their spiritual life, or their relational life, lead them to find shelter in you. For those of us who can reach out to help, give us insights about what to do, courage to get involved, and the wisdom to know when the best thing needed is our prayers and possibly our witness. Amen

March 6

Strong God of Truth, we are content to live with lies or partial truths. We proclaim them as if they have come directly from you. We delude ourselves with believing that we know your mind and fathom your ways. We forget the words that you uttered to Job, "Where were you when I laid the foundation of the earth? Tell me, if you have understanding....Have you commanded the morning since your days began, and caused the dawn to know its place, so that it might take hold of the skirts of the earth, and the wicked be shaken out of it?...Do you give the horse its might? Do you clothe its neck with mane?...Is it by your wisdom that the hawk soars, and spreads its wings toward the south?" Holy One, give us humility. Enable us to listen to others so that together we may share our bits of truth and come closer to knowing the truths that you desire for us. Enlighten us for the living of our days. Amen

—From

Job 38:4,12; 39:16,26

March 7

God of Mystery, how is it that I am most aware that you are here when things go wrong or when nothing is turning out as I've prayed for? Is it that I don't remember that I need you when things are going well? Are you there and I just don't look for you because everything is fine, just fine? Is there another way for me to remember to reach out to you without bad things happening? That's up to me? Oh…oh…oh. Thank you, most present God, for reminding me of this reality. Amen

March 8

God of Earth, Air, Height, and Depth, our world seems to be falling apart. Earthquakes, floods, storms, wars, hunger, and homelessness—just to name a few—make us wonder if you've finally given up on us. Or maybe we've given up on ourselves? Maybe we don't fully understand how magnificent, how compassionate, how creative you've created us to be. Maybe we'd rather blame you for the state of our world than accept that we're the ones who are responsible for a lot of the mess that's here. Shake us out of our complacency. Instill in us your fire for righteousness in our world. May we become the answers to the prayers we make. Amen

March 9

Great God Our Hope, when you shake us out of our comfortable ruts, thank you for giving us hope as we reluctantly let go of our lethargy. Thank you for giving us messengers from you who encourage us to walk in unknown paths. We praise you that you love us enough to let us not be satisfied with who we are but always pull us to be more fully the people you are calling us to be. Amen

March 10

Our Creator and Our Teacher, thank you for people who want to learn. We all want to remain ignorant in our lives...some in one area and others in another. It takes courage to be willing to move beyond our comfortable ways of thinking. Because you open us to new ways, we thank you...even when we'd rather stay ignorant. Amen

March 11

Healer of the Sick, we lift up all those who are suffering in body or spirit. When we feel helpless to relieve their pain, all we know to do is give them to you. Why is that our *last* resort rather than our *first*?

We ask that you guide the hands, heads, and hearts of those who tend to others. Guide their interventions so that healing occurs. Even if a cure is not possible, may those who suffer experience wholeness in their spirits that they may have never had. Give them awareness that they are not alone, they are loved, and life is still good. Amen

March 12

God of Wisdom, I wonder what in the world happened. She and I were involved in the same event but she saw it one way and I saw it differently. How is that possible? Were we in alternate realities like in science fiction movies? This stark difference in our understanding shook the ground under me. Do these differences happen more than I'm aware? Is this part of your intervention in my lethargic way of looking at things in life? If so, I guess I need to thank you for this kind of shake up that causes me to grow in ways that were unimaginable to me before. However, I'm not really ready to be fully grateful yet. Amen

March 13

"What's up?" If every time we talked, God, I began our chats with these words, "What's up?" how would that be? A lot of people begin conversations that way. So, what's up, God? Somehow, that just does not seem right. It does not seem holy enough. Addressing the creator of the universe with "What's up?" just seems weak.

But what if you greeted me each morning and night with "What's up?" Wow!!! Then I have to consider my day in terms of what's important to share with you. Have I done anything that I'd be proud to let you in on? Have I been the kind of person you created me to be? Have I exhibited the love of Jesus with everyone in my life? "What's up?" What have I done to uplift? What have I done that put someone down? Have I been more involved with doing than being? Have I taken care of urgent things and ignored important ones? "What's up?" Help me with being able to answer this question in ways that I am not ashamed of.

And by the way, the next time I ask someone "What's up?" help me really listen. And if they ask me "What's up?" and then don't pay attention when I answer, give me patience and understanding to love them…no matter what…just like you love me. Amen

March 14

"Spirit of the living God, Fall afresh on me;…Melt me, Mold me, Fill me, Use me. Spirit of the living God, fall afresh on me." Amen

—From

Daniel Iverson, "Spirit of the Living God", The Presbyterian Hymnal, Westminster/John Knox Press: Louisville, KY, 1990, p 322.

March 15

Holy God, sometimes I just don't want to pray. I want to curl up in bed, pull up the covers, and ignore the world and everything that's in it. I hope that's okay. Amen

March 16

God of Amazing Discoveries, once again John Bell's book, *There Is One Among Us?*, caught my eye as it sits on the shelf above my computer. Except today I don't even want to open it. The title makes me wonder: How does knowing that there is one among us—whoever or whatever that one might be—change how I live my life? Is there one...saint? One...liar? One...angel? One...thief? How does that affect what you want from me? Amen

—From

John L. Bell, There Is One Among Us, GIA Publications, Inc.: Chicago, IL, 1999

March 17

God of Mercy, be merciful to me and all the rest of us. As much as we like to delude ourselves into how wonderful each of us is, we know, in our hearts, that simply is not so. So please be merciful. Keep leading us into being the people you intend us to be. Amen

March 18

Okay, Lord. I just get so frustrated with people who truly believe they are self-made. Do they use computers in their work? Probably. Did they create the software they depend on to run their business? Probably not. How did they learn what they know? Did they have teachers? Did they have access to capital of some sort? None of us is truly self-made. When will we stop lying? I guess that we really give you a good laugh when we pull out that "self-made" card. Amen

March 19

God of Forgiveness, you know that time in the worship services of some churches when people read together the printed Prayer of Confession? Who comes up with those things? Only occasionally are the words appropriate for me. When that happens, they actually punch me pretty hard with concepts I've ignored or deluded myself with. But many times, I just read the words with everyone else because that's what I'm supposed to do.

I admit that I like congregational prayers of confession that are followed by a time of silence when we can offer our own private prayers. Even then sometimes I draw a blank. I can't think of anything to verbalize as confession. I guess I could always pray, "God, I'm feeling good about myself and so suspect that I have blind spots I'm ignoring. Stay with me as I begin to notice those things that I need to." And yet, other times, I begin praying in my head and hardly get going good before the prayer leader says "Amen".

I guess that he or she didn't have a lot to confess that day. Maybe they could leave us a little more time for whatever pops into our heads during the time of silence? Anyway, I just needed to confess my ambivalence about prayers of confession. Mind you, I'm not opposed to confession. I think it's good for the soul because it means that you have opened my eyes and heart to something that you want me to pay attention to. So, Loving and Forgiving God, help me to be truly confessional to you, my creator, redeemer, and comforter. Amen

March 20

Joyous God, heard any good jokes lately? You've pulled off some good ones in the past. Remember when Sarah laughed when she learned she was going to have a baby—even when she knew she was already old—too old to have a baby? That was a good one. And what about when you talked about a camel going through the eye of a needle? What a crazy picture! Oh yeah, how about when Balaam's donkey started talking? Or when you turned water into the wine after everyone had already been partying at the wedding for quite a time. You sure know how to liven up a situation. Help us always to look for the laughter in life. Your gift of humor helps us transcend the everyday to catch a glimpse of you. Thanks. And oh yeah…have you heard the one about…. Amen

March 21

Conqueror of Evil, there is so much evil in the world. How do we make sense of it and believe in you as well? Do you allow evil? Do you punish it? Are you a judge? Are you all-loving, no matter how horrendous the action? Are you with us even in evil's midst? Thinkers of past and present wrestle with evil and you. Is there a way to wrap our rational minds around what seems so irrational and draconian? What do we do with evil? For now, all I can do is bring my fears and doubts to you. I trust your love and your powers to redeem evil. In the resurrection you demonstrated that you could conquer even death. Sometimes it would be nice to have a little more clarity about how you and evil relate. Maybe later? Amen

March 22

God of Resurrection, when we walk through Advent, we eagerly anticipate birth. However, when we walk through Lent, we know that we are walking toward death. Be with us and continually remind us that after crucifixion is resurrection.

Even with this resurrection hope, we know that many are struggling with death. We ask for your grace and love to surround…

Those who are living with a chronic illness;

Those who know their time on this earth is brief because of illness or age;

Those who wish they *could* die because of trauma or crises in their lives;

Those who are experiencing the death of a marriage, a career, or a dream;

Those who are grieving loss of precious people;

Those who are in crucifying situations in their lives;

Those who are letting go of one way of being and moving toward another way.

O Life of All Who Live, we turn to you as our hope, our joy, our comfort, and our praise. Challenge us to be present with each other in times of death—whether that death is literal or figurative—so that we can manifest your grace and love. In the assurance of the new life of resurrection we pray. Amen

March 23

Great God Our Hope, we thank you that we can turn to you in times of uncertainty—whether that time of discomfort is *personal* as with our families and careers or *public* as in our country or local community.

We place ourselves in the surety of your presence and care —even when all evidence sometimes points in other directions.

God of all goodness, we bring to you our joys:

Our delight in children as they gleefully discover the wonders of a caterpillar

> The amazement of flushing toilets
>
> The thrill of a driver's permit
>
> Our satisfaction in jobs done well and on time
>
> Our mutuality of relationships

We exult in music, art, colorful trees, and freshly pressed linen. We are comforted by the twinkle of wrinkled eyes of parents and grandparents as they share themselves through stories. We enjoy the pleasure of soaking baths and freshly mopped kitchen floors.

(continued)

Merciful God, we bring to you also our disappointments, our challenges, our failures, our frustrations. We ask that you help us find wisdom in our trials and growth in our mistakes. Help us not to define ourselves and our world by the bad but to use the bad to redirect our lives for fresh meaning and undiscovered possibility. We ask you to open our eyes in new ways so that we may be aware of your presence and be undergirded by your care.

We have nothing without your love, guidance, grace, and wisdom. Help us to claim your gifts to us and use them for our community in ways that are pleasing to you. We pray in hope, joy, and peace. Amen

March 24

Generous Provider of All Good Gifts,

I thank you for the many blessings that you give to me:

Mountains that lift my eyes upward

Rivers that sing to my soul

Trees that delight me with their colors

People who remind me of the vast diversity of your creation

Pets who soothe me when I'm stressed

God of the Loving Heart,

Give me the will to show my gratitude by caring for all the beautiful world you have given to me.

Give me the guts to do what needs to be done even when doing so is difficult.

Give me the heart to love even when I do not want to.

Give me the hands to reach out in service even when I'd rather put them in my pockets.

Give me the tear to feel the pain of others.

Most merciful God, I thank you for the many people in my community who live in wise and caring ways, who work for what is right, and who challenge the rest of us to be part of the solutions. Amen

March 25

Holy God, Who is Both Change and Changelessness,

Give us courage to make the changes needed in our community so that everyone who lives here can become truly the person you intend him or her to be.

Give us wisdom to hold fast to honor, honesty, compassion, and creativity.

Holy God, Who is Both Patience and Impatience,

Give us the desire for patience for the long journey required for our community to reflect justice and mercy for everyone.

Give us the will to push and push and push so that those who are invisible in our community can enjoy the benefits offered here.

Holy God, Who is Both Love and Judgment,

Give us open hearts to love those who anger us, challenge us, frustrate us, or hurt us.

Give us support to name the deceptions that motivate our decisions.

Holy God, Who is Both Personal to the Individual and Communal to the World,

Give us faith to call you to our innermost beings.

Give us vision to look beyond self-interest.

(continued)

Holy God, Who is Both Giver and Receiver,

Give us the joy of acknowledging to you the many benefits of your love and your inspiration.

Give us grateful hearts for the many blessings we enjoy, especially for fellowship, food, and celebration of this day. Amen

March 26

Great God of Wonder, Undergird us with your steadfast love and fill me with hope. We look around and see pain, touch frustration, hear despair, and feel struggle. When we witness the darkness of the lives of people in our communities, we need help that can come only from your divine source. We need your energy, discernment, and wisdom as we walk alongside people who are hurting. Help us stay focused on their needs and to be instruments of your grace and healing.

Merciful God, we seek to change our communities for all citizens who live and work here. Help us to love you with *all* our strength, *all* our minds, *all* our hearts, and *all* our souls, and to truly choose to love our neighbors as ourselves. Amen

March 27

Holy God of Compassion, we have people in our community and our world for whom Psalm 69 accurately describes their situation. They cry: "Save me, O God, for the waters have come up to my neck. I sink in deep mire, where there is no foothold; I have come into deep waters, and the flood sweeps over me. I am weary with my crying; my throat is parched. My eyes grow dim with waiting for my God. More in number than the hairs of my head are those who hate me without cause; many are those who would destroy me, my enemies who accuse me falsely. What I did not steal must I now restore?" Help us be instruments of your saving grace for them. Lead us to lift them up with justice and mercy. Keep us mindful that our neighbors ache and that you expect us to respond by sharing your love in tangible and graceful ways. Amen

—From

Psalm 69:1-4

March 28

God of Joy, thank you for people who are able to laugh at things that happen in their lives—things that anger others. I'm talking about those people who can see the humor in a broken treasure, a burned meal, or a spilled glass of milk. Help us learn from them that much of what we agonize over is truly funny—when we can get a little perspective. Remind us that a dirty floor that we just finished mopping really does not matter in the long view of history. Open our eyes to the joy of living and give us laughter at outrageous, unexpected turns. Amen

March 29

Watchful and Caring God, be vigilant for those people who hurt deep inside but no one knows of their pain. Hold them in your loving embrace especially when they cannot experience it because of their situation. Surround them with people who are able to offer graceful words and actions just because that's what they do—without knowing the powerful impact of their love. Sustain suffering people to the point they can finally reach out to others who can empathize with their agony. Help people in pain begin to experience some support and relief. Thank you for your persistent care of each of us. Without it, what would we do? Amen

March 30

My friend James once said, "The battle is not mine; it's the Lord's." Help me remember his words of wisdom. Amen

March 31

Most Loving God, today I use words from St. Teresa of Avila to pray. She wrote:

> "Let nothing disturb you,
>
> Let nothing frighten you,
>
> All things pass away:
>
> God never changes.
>
> Patience obtains all things.
>
> He who has God
>
> Finds he lacks nothing;
>
> God alone suffices." Amen

—From

http://thecorner.typepad.com/bc/2008/09/teresa-of-avila.htm web search 10.16.12

April 1

God of Fools, today is the day when people play practical jokes on others. And yet, according to the Apostle Paul, you "chose what is foolish in the world to shame the wise;...[you] chose what is weak in the world to shame the strong." How is it that we get so entranced with people who seem so worldly wise and in charge and yet you choose those who seem least likely to speak your truth? Clog up our ears and hearts so we can ignore those voices that speak only for themselves. Open our ears and hearts so we can hear those who speak *your* truth. Amen

—From
I Cor. 1:27

April 2

Holy God of Blessedness, you have said that the poor in spirit will receive the kingdom of heaven. When I think of poor, I think about people who don't have adequate resources. But that's not necessarily who you're talking about, is it? You're talking about people who know that without you, they are nothing. They have value only because of you in their lives. They are poor in spirit because they know that *your* grace, *your* love, *your* joy, *your* faith, and *your* mercy are what sustain them. Most Loving Savior, help me be poor in spirit. Amen

—From
Matthew 5:3

April 3

God of Those Who Mourn, you have said that mourners will be comforted. Thank you for being with those who suffer personal loss of some kind. But do you mean more than that? Do you mean that your followers are to mourn what happens to our fellow human beings? That we are to feel their griefs and losses as intensely as we feel our own? And when and if we acknowledge their mourning, who is to comfort them? Me? Us? You mean that's how you expect comfort to happen…for our arms to embrace those who hurt? For our resources to be shared to meet their need? For our compassion to let them know they are not alone? Oh my, I pray that you will move us to notice those who mourn and then move us to be your comforters to them. Amen

—*From*
Matthew 5:4

April 4

God of the Meek, I'm sorry but I just don't want to be meek. I want to stand up and be counted. I want to fight for what is right, especially for what's right for me. I want to be strong, vocal, and stubborn. I can still be those things and be meek? How in the world do you figure that one? Sure, I remember Aristotle but you need to remind me what he said that is important for this conversation. He said something about meekness being the center point between too much anger and too little? Well, that makes sense. So being meek is about the strength of Gandhi or the vision of Martin Luther King, Jr.? It's about honoring others, even when we don't agree with them or even like them? It's about standing up for justice when we're not sure of the outcome but know we have to abide in your commitment to justice? So when you help us to be meek, you say that we will inherit the earth? Is that because we will not expect anything? Therefore, what you provide will be a wonderful, huge, totally surprising gift? That's something to think about. Amen

—*From*

Matthew 5:5

April 5

God of Those Who Hunger and Thirst after Righteousness, I'm not sure that I know anyone like this...people who are starving for social justice to happen. Yes, I know people who would appreciate someone noticing their unjust personal situation. I know people who actively work on justice issues and try to provide the basic needs their neighbors need. But to hunger and thirst? To feel so passionate that you feel as if you've been wandering in the desert for days with only a few sips of water to get you through? To be so hungry for balance in the lives of others in our world that you would eat almost anything to survive? That kind of commitment and passion may be asking a lot, you know? And yet, you say that when we want justice so badly that we feel it as a physical ache, we are filled. That's amazing, God! Sometimes that assurance is important for the journey of working for others, for confronting what St. Paul calls the "powers and principalities," and for when we experience more failures and mistakes than successes. Thank you for your blessings. Please keep them coming. We surely need them. Amen

—From
Matthew 5:6

April 6

God of Mercy, you have taught us that when we are merciful, we receive mercy. You know how badly we want and need your mercy. We mess up all the time and so your steadfast love is important to our being able to keep going each day. But do we really have to be merciful in return? Really? Isn't there some wiggle room there? No? Well, help us soften our hearts so that we can share your magnificent gift to everyone. Amen

—From
Matthew 5:7

April 7

God of Rich Blessings, you have taught that when we are pure in heart, we will see God. Maybe I've seen too many science fiction movies to truly embrace wanting to see you. I remember that even Moses fell down when he realized that he was seeing you as a burning bush. On the other hand, to be able to experience closeness with you through the sense of sight would have to be awesome.

So then what do you mean about purity of heart? I know that in ancient times, the heart was the abode of the will. Do you mean that we are to have purity of will? If so, that's a tall order. I might want to do something good as a witness to faith in you, but you know me. You know there's always a piece of me that hopes I'll get something good out of my good deeds. You know that as much as I want to do your will fully, I still hold back. You know that others may believe I'm exemplary in my actions, but that there is always an underlying motivation, belief, or desire that does not honor you.

Please forgive me for my lack of purity of heart. Lead me to strive to align my will with yours. And please, please let me always experience your presence with me in whatever way that occurs. Amen

—*From*

Matthew 5:8

April 8

God of Shalom, you promised blessings to peacemakers, not peacekeepers. Peacemakers do whatever it takes to bring about peace. However, peacekeepers do not shake the status quo. They may deny that there is discord within their community. They smooth over significant conflicts, hoping that being nice will win the day. Peacekeepers may not ask those difficult questions involving "why?"

Holy God of Peace, give me courage to be a peacemaker. Your promise is that I will be called one of your children. That's a blessing I want to claim, Most Loving And Gracious Lord. Amen

—From

Matthew 5:9

April 9

Okay God, this is a difficult one. You have taught that we are blessed when we are persecuted for righteousness sake, when we are reviled, and when people utter all kinds of evil against us for your sake. What is this? Oh, I get it. You are not asking us to do anything that Jesus did not do. You promise that the kingdom of heaven will be ours. All this sounds like a challenge that is overwhelming. But you assure us that with you, all things are possible. So we're counting on you. And you're counting on us. Is that a covenant? Help us to fulfill our end of the bargain because we believe that you will do as you have said. Thanks for your help. Amen

—From
Matthew 5:10-11

April 10

God of Love, you have called us to love you totally…with all our heart, mind, soul, and strength and our neighbor as ourselves. I need to meditate with you about all this. So today, can we chat about loving you with our heart? Heart is how we often describe our emotions as in "I love you with all my heart."

The ancients thought of the heart as the place of will. Therefore, when we love you with all our heart, we decide (*will*) to love you with all our emotions—love, fear, shame, hate, joy, elation, or despair. You mean that you can handle all of those feelings, especially the ones that we don't want to feel? We can actually hate you at times and you will still love us? Amazing! That's a little intimidating to think that I can love you with every emotion I feel. What a total kind of connection! Thank you for wanting that kind of wholeness from me. Amen

—From
Mark 12:29-31

April 11

Most Loving Creator, Redeemer, and Sustainer, I want to love you with my mind. In some ways, this kind of love may be the easiest because I am a thinker by nature. And yet, my thoughts lead to paths that end up tangled or with unacceptable conclusions. I *think* based on what I *already* know, have experienced, or been told by people I respect. It seems to me that loving you with my mind means that I have to be willing to move beyond all those boundaries of safety and to move where you crash into my preconceptions. I have to be willing to be pushed by you to thoughts that at first do not make sense. You can open my mind in ways beyond my rational ways of processing and certainly beyond my most vivid imaginings. I'm a bit scared of this journey and yet yearn for deeper ways of knowing you and being in relationship with you. Open my mind so that I can more fully and truly love you. Amen

—*From*
Mark 12:29-31

April 12

Holy God, Lover of My Soul, how do I love you with *my* soul? Is praying a way of opening my soul to you? What about listening to other people who speak words that I hear as your own words to me? Do I connect my soul to your wondrous grace by being still and "floating" with whatever thoughts or ideas emerge? Does loving you with my soul mean that I move into the depths of my own reality—those deep places I embrace as well as those that repulse me? Do I offer the totality of me to you? Is it possible that you really can accept all of me…you know…ALL? Lord God, I sincerely hope so because I want to love you with my soul. Amen

—From

Mark 12:29-31

April 13

God of Strength, you call us to love you with our physical selves. Our bodies are your temple and you expect us to take care of them. But you know how we dishonor our bodies. We eat food that is not nutritious or healthy. We sit around and do not move our bodies. We do risky things that can hurt us. We ignore signs of overwork or increasing stress. We push, push, push trying to do more, more, more. We focus on our exteriors and ignore our interiors where our strength resides. Forgive us for not paying attention so that we can better serve and love you. Keep reminding us that you gave us bodies for strength and service. Help us to honor and care for that gift. Amen

—From
Mark 12:29-31

April 14

God Who Knew Me in My Mother's Womb, you have loved me from before I was born. You love me even when I feel unworthy. You love me when I cannot love myself. Help me to claim your love of me so that I can truly love myself…as I am. Amen

April 15

Lord God, today in the United States is the deadline for submitting taxes. It seems appropriate that in addition to praying that I grow in loving you with my heart, mind, soul, and strength that I pray about loving my neighbor as myself. I know there are many ways to love my neighbor. Today I meditate on how paying my taxes can be one way of loving my neighbor. I know that my tax money gets used for many things that I disapprove of. And yet, my taxes enable children to be educated, hungry people to be fed, sick people to receive medical care, elderly people to receive comfort, homeless people to find services that can help, and human service agencies to have funds to help people change their lives. My taxes help keep our roads safe, my garbage collected, my water regulated, and my prescriptions safe. We are to love our neighbors. Paying taxes is one way of helping to care for others who live in our country. Help us to embrace all the ways that we can show our care of others and then motivate us to *do it*! Amen

—From
Mark 12:29-31

April 16

God of the Prophets, Micah reminded us that you want us to do justice, love kindness, and walk humbly with you. Can't we just come to church once a month or so? Or how about putting money in the offering plate every so often? Why do I have to do these things? That sounds like some kind of significant commitment on my part. I think I may need some convincing and redirection of what I focus on. How about it? Amen

—From
Micah 6:6-8

April 17

Okay, so now we talk about doing justice. I thought that courts of law handled that—you know, justice. But you want us to do justice as you define it. You want us to put things into balance, to work for harmony, and to name those things that are unjust. You expect us to help those who are powerful to deepen their understanding of injustice so that the powerless have what they need. For those of us with voices that people listen to, you want us to speak for shalom balance in this world. For those of us who are never listened to, you want us to be seen and not ignored.

Holy God, we can be your people only with your guidance, patience, and training. Please lead us to be justice people. Amen

—From

Micah 6:6-8

April 18

God of Steadfast Love, thank you for asking us to love as you love…steadfastly. We confess that our love is haphazard at best. We love well when things are going how we want. We love poorly, if at all, when we are not getting our way. Our selfishness and self-centeredness lead us away from your loving kindness, constancy, and overwhelming grace. Be with us as we learn to love as you would have us to. Amen

April 19

Upholder of the Falling, you lead us to walk humbly with you. I understand the words but do you realize how hard this is to do? When I'm on top of the world and when things are going my way, humility of any kind is hard. It's especially difficult to admit that the good things are from you when I've worked so hard on my part. But walking humbly with you makes so much sense when I stop and think. When I stop….When I….When…That's you peeking around when I stop to pay attention. Please lead me in a humility walk, especially when I'm *so-o-o* not in that mindset. Amen

—From
Micah 6:6-8

April 20

God of the Resurrection, even though the date we remember your crucifixion and celebrate your resurrection moves around, this month is when we proclaim loudly, "Jesus Christ is risen today. Alleluia!" Because of this phenomenal event, we know that nothing can separate us from your love. We know that no matter what, you can make things new. What glory, what mystery, what power! All praise to you, Risen Lord. Amen

April 21

God of Health and Strength, we acknowledge that sometimes things do not go the way we want them to.

Babies are born dead or with significant health issues.

Grown children are victims of lies or cruel deaths.

Long planned futures explode with unexpected diagnoses.

Dreams for loved ones are snatched by other realities.

Jobs are lost.

Traffic accidents happen.

At those times, speak in a voice that we can hear that you are still here. We need affirmation that you are a God of health and strength. We seek assurance that you will provide us with people who can embody your love for us at this time. Make us the answers to the prayers we make. Amen

April 22

God of Beauty, thank you for daffodils, dogwood trees, tulips, violets, forsythia, azaleas, and iced tea. I suppose a non-Southerner might be grateful for other things. But this is where you have planted me and I am moved by your beautiful gifts. Your love is overwhelming in its diversity and glory. Amen

April 23

God of Comfort, there are many things in this world that I just do not understand. Cancer is one of those. It comes in many forms and its destructiveness can be excruciating—physically, psychologically, and emotionally. It jolts everyone who knows the person who has been attacked.

Thank you for helping researchers find new ways to deal with the disease. I appreciate all the medical team members who work with people who are wrestling with this demon. I'm grateful that there are chaplains and therapists who listen, console, and sometimes even conduct funerals for people who have been unlucky enough to get caught in the eye of the cancer storm. I also acknowledge that through their struggle with cancer, some people gain amazing cures for their souls and emotional healings that were profound and powerful. They are grateful for that particular aspect of what this disease brought them. I acknowledge that some cancers that lurk in our world may be caused by the damage we have done to our planet and to the things that are important for human life.

(continued)

I know all this. And still...I hate cancer. I hate the fear it brings, the uncertainties it causes, the pain it calls forth, and the financial toll that it can have. I hate losing friends and family to cancer. I despise the terror of watching someone struggle with the disease even when they conquer this monster. God, sometimes cancer is hard to reconcile with your loving grace. It becomes challenging to believe that you are here in the midst of the pain and fear. And yet, sometimes your presence—even when it seems nonexistent—is all I can hold onto. Never let my fear win. Always show your love in great and subtle ways. Support the caregivers. Most importantly surround those dealing with cancer with hope and confidence that you are with them now and in their future, whatever it may be. Amen

April 24

Radiant and Glorious God, you are with us in the depths of our despair and in the heights of our exultation. You are with us when life is boring and ordinary. You are with us when we are so filled with joy we can hardly keep our feet on the ground. Thanks for being our ground and our sky. Help us always remember that you are as close as our breath and as vast as the universe and beyond. Let us bask in your care. Amen

April 25

God, I don't know how you do it. You allow us to make mistakes. You allow us to do stupid things. You watch us be foolish, careless, or irresponsible. When I see people I care about doing these things, I get agitated, angry, or want to jump in and tell them how to live their lives. That's not how you seem to work. And yet, you obviously are in our lives, guiding us to learn from our mistakes. When we don't get it the first time, you create other opportunities for us to grow in maturity and understanding. So I just don't understand how all this works together for good. But somehow it does. God of Growth, please stay close because I'm pretty sure that I'm going to mess up again. Amen

April 26

God, Support of the Innocent, many people suffer through no fault of their own. Enflame our outrage so that we will defend those who are guiltless. Force us to see and acknowledge the victimization that happens in our own homes, communities, and world. Give us boldness to charge like mother bears to protect and defend the defenseless. Undergird our reluctance to get involved with reminders of your dying to save us. Help us claim your resurrection truths as we reach out to right injustices. We are powerless without you. Amen

April 27

Strength of All Who Labor, some in our community do not have jobs. Not only can they not support their families, they struggle to keep up their hope, sense of worth, and motivation for caring. Help our leaders find ways to open the doors to jobs for those who seek them and may those jobs create enough income to pay for basic human needs. Help those with jobs to share as they are able with those who struggle. Help all of us to know that we are part of one community, that what hurts one of us hurts all of us, and what helps one of us can improve the lives of all. Holy God, help us honor all kinds of labor. Help us create opportunities for those who desperately want and need to work. Amen

April 28

God of Abundance, some of us have too much while others of us have too little. We are seduced by luxury or stunted by poverty. Those of us who have too much do not even realize that we have enough. We are blinded by our consumption. We don't know when we are full. Most Loving Savior, help us know when enough is enough. Amen

April 29

Holy Lord Who Called the Children Forth, help us nurture children who are both smart and compass-sionate, who are winners as well as cooperative, who incorporate a strong sense of self along with commitment to community, who see the big picture and value the beautiful details of life, who acknowledge their own weaknesses and encourage the strengths of others, who adore logic and embrace miracles, and who claim life and despise cruelty. Let children cherish the differences among humans and fight against all things discriminatory. Guide them to show us the way to your kingdom. We yearn for the day when little children shall lead us because they are so closely in tune with the song you place in their hearts.

God, help us to raise children who care. Amen

April 30

Most Loving God, we come to you with mixed motives. We ask that you guide us to care for and help people who are in need. We confess that we want to help without any inconvenience or sacrifice on our part. We want all people to live in harmony and love but not if it means we have to give a little on our closely held beliefs and concepts. We yearn for every person in our community to have opportunity to become self-reliant. However, we prefer that their self-reliance come with no accommodation on our part.

Holy One for Peace, help us to see joy in service where before we saw inconvenience. Give us openness to hear another's portion of the truth because our reality is incomplete, too. Lead us to flexibility so that we can bend to another's needs. Give us loving hearts and willing minds to work, live, and play so that all may know your grace. Amen

May 1

God of Creation, Howard Thurmond said, "Don't ask yourself what the world needs; ask yourself what makes you come alive. And then go and do that. Because what the world needs is people who have come alive." I trust that what makes me come alive is following your lead for my particular path. Let me listen and follow with joy and enthusiasm, even when I'm not sure where we together are headed. Amen

—From

http://www.beliefnet.com/Quotes/Inspiration/H/Howard-Thurman/Dont-Ask-Yourself-What-The-World-Needs-Ask-Yours.aspx web search 10.17.12

May 2

God of Great Ideas, thank you for people who have gone before us and lead us even today. St. Augustine's guidance is: "Hope has two daughters: their names are anger and courage. Anger that things are the way they are. Courage to make them the way they ought to be." Give me anger and courage in the dosage that is correct for me today. Amen

—From

http://thinkexist.com/quotation/hope-has-two-beautiful-daughters-their-names-are/762510.html web search 10.17.12

May 3

God of Love, thank you for St. John of the Cross who wrote: "Where there is no love, put love—and you will find love." What a simple and yet powerful way to urge me to shine your love on everyone I meet and everywhere I go. Infuse me with your love so I may follow St. John's guidance. Amen

—From

http://www.goodreads.com/quotes/243957-where-there-is-no-love-put-love-and-you

web search 10.17.12

May 4

Is it okay to call you God of Confusion? Sometimes life just does not make sense. I think things are going one way and then they don't. I am convinced that I have the solution for what a group is wrestling with and then everything falls apart. I believe that my life is finally on the right track and then something destabilizes me. I guess that's what a lot of your followers in the Bible had happen. Mary discovered that she was going to have a baby in very unusual circumstances. The people left Egypt and wandered for forty years in the wilderness so that the original escapees left probably died along the way and only their children and grandchildren entered the land of promise. Peter and John were minding their own fishing business when you came walking by and changed their lives and history forever. So is it alright to be confused? Help me trust that you are with me and will help me muddle through until the way becomes clearer. Amen

May 5

Holy God, Shekinah, how did the children of Israel know that the cloud they were following in the desert was you? How did they realize your presence? When is a cloud not just a cloud? I'll have to listen for your guidance on this one and be comfortable with the unknowing for a time. Amen

May 6

God of New Beginnings, this month is a time for graduations. Students have completed their tasks and now are ready to march across a stage to receive a piece of paper that recognizes their accomplishments. They believe that they have finished when they are just beginning a new phase of their lives.

Where they find confusion, give them clarity for the next first step.

Where they find fear, give them confidence that they have skills and gifts to depend on.

Where they find despair, give them hope because this will pass.

Where they find joy, give them exuberance to relish the moment because this too will pass.

Where they find opportunity, give them wisdom to discern if it is for them.

Where they find relationship, give them friendships and partnerships that nurture health and growth.

Be with each of the graduates as they need. Surround them with your care and where appropriate, help us to be there to open doors to their futures. Amen

May 7

God of All Peoples, we enjoy the plumage of birds: red, yellow, browns, blacks, purples, and all kinds of mixtures of these and other colors. Why is it that skin variations matter so much and we cannot enjoy all the varieties of hues? Why do we ascribe attributes based on skin color, eye shape, hair texture, or language accent? Why can't we glory in the beauty of your creation? Why must we categorize your children in all the ways we do? Why must we label so that we can know who we like and who we don't? What is it about us? I'm not sure that I want to know that answer but I'll try to keep listening. Amen

May 8

Jesus, on occasion I see paintings of you laughing. Imprint this aspect of your presence in my life. Let me connect with the joy that you experience when you interact with us, your brothers and sisters. Help me to laugh with all my body and share your delight in humanity and all of your creation. Thank you for the gift of deep and cleansing laughter. Amen

May 9

God Who Is Present in the Darkness, let me feel your presence when I shut my eyes. If that cannot happen at this moment, send someone to me; give me words in a book, on a television show, or in an e-mail; or lift up a song that lets me know you are close. I already know your intimacy in my head but I yearn to feel it in my soul. Amen

May 10

God of Ministry, today I pray for all ministers. Feed their souls so that they can feed their flocks with real spiritual food and not junk snacks. Engage their minds so they can learn from you, the Master, rather than spouting the current religious jargon. Give them humility so they can serve as you need rather than trying to be the Messiah themselves. Help them honor themselves with spiritual, physical, and emotional rest. Inspire their joy, imaginations, and zest for living so that they do not give up on the call to ministry that you instilled in their hearts. Be with them, Lord, for they need you. Amen

May 11

God of Mystery, there is so much I do not understand. Why is my life relatively stable and others' lives are not? Why do some people seem to thrive on chaos while others demand calm and serenity? Why are some people content with what they have, no matter how little that may be, and others crave more and more even though they have excess abundance? Why do some people desire control and other people will not accept responsibility of any kind? Why are some people full of joy even in the worst circumstances while others are gloomy and morose almost all the time? Why are some people able to shake off disappointment while others seethe with anger and resentment?

God, you made all of us. That's hard for me to accept about some people but I know it is true. Help me embrace myself and others with your love, grace, and mercy even when I can't see your work in my or their lives. Amen

May 12

Holy God, who are you? Where are you? What are you doing? Are you there? I'm praying to you so I must believe. Do I really? Help me. Amen

May 13

Companion of the Lonely, be with those who feel that no know cares about them or even knows they exist. Because they are invisible to most of us, we don't reach out. Because we are busy with our own lives, we do not seek out people who feel they have no place on this earth. We ignore those who believe they are just taking up space on the planet. Forgive us.

Make us aware of people who need you to touch them by using our human hands and hearts. Help us find ways to reach those who do not exist in our reality but nevertheless are your beloved children.

Most Loving God, when we ourselves are in that dark and lonely place, lead people to us as well. As we want for us, let us offer to others. Amen

May 14

Source of Blessing, thank you for garbage collectors…those who take away our trash from homes, businesses, and streets. They keep us healthy and give us pride in our surroundings. Thank you, too, for those people who take our emotional, spiritual, and psychological garbage and help us sift through it so we can keep what is helpful and throw away what is truly trash in our lives. Help us honor all those people who exist to make our lives easier. Let us never take them for granted. Amen

May 15

Most Holy God, you are to be praised and glorified. You are beyond my imagining and your ways are not my ways. You know me and you still love me. You created the universe and beyond—all that is—and yet you care about the smallest details in my life and in the lives of everyone and everything that lives. My heart overflows with love as I try to fathom your greatness. Alleluia. Amen

May 16

God of Straight Ways, thank you for lanes on highways. Most vehicles use them well, keeping us safe and on the straight and narrow. When everyone is rushing, rushing, rushing, and driving fast, fast, fast, the comfort of those two lines is tremendous.

I wish that I had a lane in my life that I could get in. I would know that as long as I stayed between the lines (and others did as well), I would get to my destination. As long as I was in the correct lane, I'd know when to turn—safely—and I'd get where I wanted to go. I know that you provide guidance through your written and spoken word but sometimes those two lines sure would be nice. Amen

May 17

Holy Spirit, Lama Surya Das in *Practicing with Loss* wrote: "We exhale, and we let go of the old moment. It is lost to us. In so doing, we let go of the person we used to be. We inhale and we breathe in the moment that is becoming. In so doing, we welcome the person we are becoming: We repeat the process. This is meditation. This is renewal. It is also life." Spirit of God, fall on me. Breathe with, through, in, and for me. Renew me. Remind me that my life is in your breath. Amen

—From

http://mindfulbalance.org/2011/11/26/this-moment-is-always-changing/ web search 1.17.12

May 18

Eternal Ruler, why is it when we disagree with a national or world leader, we use you to justify our opinion? We find something that person did and then hold it up as proof that they are against you or for you, depending on our viewpoint? When did it become so easy for us to think we can manipulate you and that you need our protection? Why do we think that rulers speak *for* or *against* you? When did it become possible for Christians or Muslims or Jews to think that someone who wants to include people of other faiths in conversations about national or world problems are against Christians, Muslims, or Jews?

Mighty God, give us patience with our rulers. Guide their decisions with your wisdom. Help us to understand that faith presents itself in different ways in different people in different times. Convince us that we do not have to agree with each other in order to be your children and followers. Lead us to demonstrate our faith through our caring for others. Convince us that you and not we are the judge of a person's rightness with you. Amen

May 19

Most Wondrous God of Vision, Marcel Proust has said: "The real voyage of discovery consists not in seeking new landscapes but in having new eyes." Please give me new eyes to see what you want me to see. Amen

—From

http://thinkexist.com/quotation/the_real_voyage_of_d iscovery_consists_not_in/144224.html

web search 10.17.12

May 20

Father, Son, and Holy Spirit, today I join with the twenty-four elders who fell before you in the book of the Revelation of John and sang, "You are worthy, our Lord and God, to receive glory and honor and power, for you created all things, and by your will they existed and were created." Amen and Amen

—From

Revelation 4:11

May 21

Ever Loving God, thank you for bringing unexpected blessings into my life. You sent the extremely well-dressed man who shared with me how a program I'd been involved with had changed his life, the hummingbird that flew by when I needed to know you were listening and the card that came just because someone was thinking of me. These treasures fill my heart.

Open my spirit to hear your nudges for me to be a source of blessing to someone even if and when I have no idea that I am your instrument of choice at the moment. Amen

May 22

Generous Provider of All Good Gifts, do you ever tire of hearing all my "I wants"? Maybe just for today, I can limit those? Maybe? Amen

May 23

Power That Saves, save me from myself when I…

Over function;

Take too much control;

Complain about someone who is actually a reflection of something I don't like in myself;

Refuse to listen to sage advice;

Disconnect from healthy living.

Surround me with people who can speak the truth to me in ways that I can hear. Open me to your guidance for living abundantly and with joy. Amen

May 24

God Who Holds Our Futures,

We sing of change
With fear and anticipation
As fact surrounding us

We sing of change
With yearning and reluctance
As unavoidable

We sing of change
With hope and anxiety

As change comes
May we embrace changes upon us
Changes in our governments
Changes in the economy
Changes in the community and our personal lives
So that we may live knowing your love and grace,
O God Who Undergirds Us In The Change. Amen

May 25

Loving God, Holy One of Our Lives, we come to you with our heads bowed in shame. We have brothers and sisters who have no place to call home who walk our streets. We choose not to see them or we decide that they want to live in dumpsters or in bamboo thickets. We wash our hands of them and we sweep our streets of them. We study the causes, make our pronouncements, write our laws, design our policies…and we forget.

Help us see you in our brothers and sisters and therein care for you love you, our God, who was yourself homeless. Lead us to be your partner in claiming our community as your holy place. Amen

May 26

God of Justice, help me to see joy in service where before I saw inconvenience. Give me openness to hear another's portion of the truth that I do not have because my reality is incomplete, too. Lead me to flexibility so that I can bend to another's needs. Give me a loving heart and willing mind to work, live, and play so that all may know your grace. Amen

May 27

God of the Downtrodden, turn us around so that we may learn from homeless people and those who are poor. Help us celebrate what they can teach us about themselves as well as about ourselves and who you are. Once we see through their eyes, sear your truth in our hearts that we may amass all the power and resources at our disposal to serve those whom you care for—those who have no power or resources. Make us aware of the unexpected ways you continue to come to us. You have revealed yourself in the past in a burning bush, a pillar of cloud, a baby in a manger, and as an itinerant rabbi…why not a ragged, smelly man who looks in our eyes? Open our hearts, minds, souls, and strength so we may love you and our neighbor as ourselves. Amen

May 28

God of the Beginning and the End, people are waiting for answers: for medical test results, dates for medical procedures, results of employment interviews, college acceptance letters, answers to a marriage proposal, did they win the lottery?, and a host of other questions. Be with them in their waiting so they can be patient. When they need to push for an answer, give them insight into how hard and when to push. When the answer is not the one they were looking for, give them courage and hope to pursue whatever is next in their lives. Always surround them with the assurance that you are with them whatever their future holds. When we need to convey your message of love and care, give us the words that you desire for them to hear in their hearts. Amen

May 29

Guardian of our Lives, thank you for people who hear about a problem and then do something about it...anonymously. Their generosity of spirit and resources reminds us in powerful ways of your magnificent care. They reach out and let us know that we are not alone. You offer truly wonderful gifts to others through your inspiration that shines through these loving people. How can our praises and gratitude even begin to address your awesome care? Amen

May 30

God of Wonders, Sonya said that she prayed every morning that those she meets will see Jesus shining through her. Let this be my prayer. Amen

May 31

God of the Past, Present, and Future, some dates on the calendar have memories that are bittersweet. A date might be the anniversary of a marriage that was full of promise and commitment but later ended in divorce. It might be the day a beloved child was born but later died prematurely. It might be the date that someone was finally released from a lingering and agonizing death but is still missed and grieved even years later. It may be the holiday that reminds us of joyful times, even though many of the family members who are part of those memories are no longer present because of distance or death. Help us remember the good parts and release the painful parts to you. Give us a gentle reminder that all of life has both highs and lows. Assure us that you are indeed with us through it all and that we are not alone. You *were* here, you *are* here now, and you *will* be here. Thanks be to you, O God. Amen

June 1

God of Wonders, thank you for people

Who have vision when everyone

      around them is blind;

Who find gratitude when it makes no sense;

Who find love amidst anger and hatred;

Who find peace in the middle of violence;

Who find joy when surrounded by sorrow.

Help those of us who cannot find evidences of you in these situations to realize that these people are not crazy. Let them become our teachers. Help *them* help *us* grow in faith, love, and grace. Amen

June 2

God of New Birth, I pray for babies. As they grow, may they…

Learn to see the beauty within people and not just what is on the outside;

Laugh and cry and feel fully all the emotions that make us human;

Be generous of spirit, time, and energy with others and with themselves;

Think for themselves, listen to their own inner wisdom, and value the insights of others;

Experience the wonder and grace of divinity and know the joy of humanness;

See greatness in small things and smallness in great things;

Learn courage and gather humility around them;

Work hard and play with abandon;

Love passionately and find those who love them without reserve.

Have a future where they receive all they need to become the people you are creating them to be. Amen

June 3

God of Abundance, help me to clean out my closets—not only my real closets but those that are inside me. In order to discern what to get rid of and what to keep, you've given me these questions, first for my real closet and then for my soul closet:

Do I really like the way I feel and look when I wear this? Do I really reflect your presence in my life when I "wear" this attitude or action?

Is this garment in good repair? Am I taking care of my spiritual life or letting it drift?

Does this garment fit me well? Does this belief or opinion fit me as a person of faith?

Does this garment make me look the way I want to look? Do I model the way Jesus taught us to live in how I go through each day?

Holy God, when the answer is "no" to any of these questions, help me to clean the garment / attitude / opinion, etc. out of my life.

Help me remember that I worship a God of plenty, not a God of scarcity. Help me claim that what I will end up with in my closet will feel and actually *be* abundant. Amen

June 4

Holy God, Proclaimer of Justice, I trust you with my lament. Are you awake?

Ordinary folks who simply worked their jobs, paid their bills, loved their children, come seeking help. Their world has fallen apart through no fault of their own.

So they come.

Political leaders, who are charged with looking after us seem out of touch, spend money on death, not life, close their eyes to long term solutions—seeking only votes.

So they don't come.

People with financial resources fear, fret, worry, fight, protect, defend and close their doors, their hearts.

So they may not come.

And yet....

People come with tears, fears,

They come with yearning, hoping,

They come with visions and nightmares.

They come looking for .... looking for.... looking for.....

Holy God, are you awake? Amen

June 5

God of Conviction, Conversion, and Consecration, Gail Godwin tells the story of "Chief Drowning Bear (c.1759-1839), who held his people firm to the old Cherokee religion in these mountains.[The chief] once allowed a Christian missionary to read several chapters of the Bible to him. After the missionary had finished, Drowning Bear remarked thoughtfully, 'It seems to be a good book—strange that the white people are not better, after having had it so long.'"

Help us live so that Drowning Bear might not say those incriminating words about us. Amen

—*From*

Gail Godwin, Evensong, Ballantine Publishing, New York, 1999, p. 214

June 6

Mighty God, why is it that when things are going well, I don't think much about you? Open my eyes, heart, ears, and mind to my tendencies to ignore the evidences of your presence in my life. Amen

June 7

Awesome God, I look out the window and see the variety of life in the world: people, plants, colors, and weather. Thank you for creating a world that is not boring, constantly changes, and always has something new to offer. You delight my soul with this variety of gifts. What a magnificent God you are. Amen

June 8

Comfort of Sufferers, thank you for sneezes. Even though allergies can be irritating…ha, ha, ha…did you get that one?...sneezes can be so cathartic. Sometimes there's just nothing better than a good sneeze or two. I am constantly amazed at how perfectly you created us humans. Who would have thought of sneezes? Only our magnificent God, creator of the world and all that is in it. Thank for this comfort—the wonderful cleansing experience of a sneeze. Amen

June 9, 2011

Light of the World, there are so many kinds of lights:

Big lights for stadiums

Street lights

Car lights

Lamps and lights for homes

Flashlights

Candles

Penlights

Which kind of light am I for you? I suspect that the beacon of your light that I shed on the world is miniscule—a penlight or even less. But I suppose that if enough of us penlights got together, we could light up a stadium. We could help the world see your awesome love, grace, peace, and joy. Keep working with all of us to expand your light in this world that sometimes seems so dark. We need you to help us see the way for life and faith. Amen

June 10

Everlasting God, today I pray for those who are losing their memories due to some kind of debilitating illness. I especially lift up those who still know that they cannot remember and are filled with frustration at their increasing inability.

Even more, Most Loving God, I pray for friends and family who are hurt when their loved one cannot remember them or share in their memories. The person they hold in their hearts and minds is slipping away from them—sometimes fast and sometimes slow. They grieve bit by bit, day by day, week by week, month by month, and year by year. Uphold them as they care for this person who looks like a precious loved one but does not bear resemblance to the person they knew. Give them strength to love each day even when that loving hurts so much or when they shut out all feelings just to get by.

Guide all of us in how to share community and fellowship with the one needing care and the one(s) giving care. Let us not shut those out of our lives simply because being with them is too challenging. Help us be a loving presence in your name. Amen

June 11

Dearest Jesus, Father God, Holy Spirit, did you say these words aloud through a human voice, in a dream, or did I simply imagine them? I really do not care how you gave this blessing to us all. We cherish it and hold to it tightly.

My blessing pours forth from my love for you.

I love your strength and I love your tenderness.

I love your focus and I love your floating.

I love your rationality and I love your intuition.

I love your adult and I love your child.

I love your groundedness and

I love your imagination.

I love your tears and I love your laughter.

I love your fear and I love your courage.

I love your closeness and I love your distance.

I love your weakness and I love your power.

I love your clarity and I love your confusion.

I love your aloneness and I love your togetherness.

I love you in faith and I love you in doubt.

I love you quiet and I love you active.

(continued)

Because I love you, I bless you in your entirety.

I bless you in your bigness.

I bless your past, your present, and your future.

You are golden.

Let your light shine before others so they may see your good works and glorify me, your Creator, Redeemer, and Sustainer.

Thank you, Yahweh. I have no other words to convey my gratitude for your overwhelming blessing. Amen

June 12

God of Wonder, gifts come in all shapes and sizes. Many of the best and most treasured are those that are not wrapped in beautiful papers and tied with fancy ribbons...

The gift of being affirmed when I'm feeling low;

The gift of a joke shared;

The gift of an unexpected invitation to do something that nurtures my soul.

We give when we offer to care for a pet so someone can travel to spend time with family or friends. We give when we prepare food for someone who is grieving. Sometimes, however, gifts are given and received with no planning, forethought, or expectation. Such gifts are truly special because they come when least expected. Lead us to be aware and full of gratitude when such gifts come our way. And especially help us to be unexpected gift givers. Amen

June 13

Holy God Who Calls Out Our Gifts For Service, thank you for the long haul truck driver who shared with me his personal ministry of caring for others. While he is out on the road, he writes articles of encouragement that appear in his church newsletter. He makes copies that he keeps in his truck. As he meets other drivers who begin to share their lives, struggles, and concerns with him, he gives them one of his articles. He tries to choose the one that most closely connects with their personal situations. He said that when he sees some of those guys again, they ask, "Got another one of those articles to give me?"

When we choose to serve you, Loving God, we are often limited by our own understandings of what we can do. We think we must teach Sunday School, sing in the choir, visit shut-ins, or volunteer in human service organizations. All of those ways to serve are important. They are wonderful ministries for people who are blessed with the gifts that enhance these special ways of serving. The truck driver reminds us that we all can serve. We all can find what brings us joy as we reach out with love and compassion to others. Help each of us to uncover that special gift you have given us to share with the world. Amen

June 14

Awesome God, thank you for the many ways you answer our prayers.

When we pray for miracles,

You gently remind us that we already have miracles in our lives in our family members—old and young.

When we pray for future outcomes,

You gracefully remind us that we have today to treasure.

When we pray for strength,

You remind us of the prayers that surround us.

When we pray for answers,

You bring the unexpected visit, e-mail, card, or phone call.

When we pray for our hurting loved ones,

You remind us of others who are devastated with pain or loss beyond our wildest imagination.

When we pray for our loss of normalcy,

You remind us that many of our neighbors count this kind of distress as normal.

God of Love,

Open our hearts to the fullness of life, with its joys and pains.

(continued)

Open our minds to the lessons you are providing us as we journey difficult roads.

Open our spirits to the unending joy of living life in you.

Open our mouths to proclaim that you are with us even when we are not sure.

Open our arms to receive the many blessings you continue to send our way.

With hope and love in your grace, we offer this prayer. Amen

June 15

God of Grace, is it true that multi-tasking and perfectionism hinder connections to your good gifts? If so, then I put up a lot of blocks to your awesome grace. In this world of bigger, better, and winning, I forget to stop and appreciate the small, the lesser, and the losing. I don't embrace the concept that enough is just right, that I am never going to be perfect but I can be just fine, and that losing is sometimes the best thing that can ever happen. I get so busy being bigger, better, and winning that I close the door to your life-giving love. How, O God, can I do this to myself? Why do I deprive myself of you, who are as close as my own breath?

I pray that you will help me embrace the awareness that I am fine just as I am, just as you have created me. I ask for your support in changing those things that you want me to change rather than trying to fit some image given to me by others: friends, family, media, or my own self. I yearn for your grace. Help me get out of my own way so I can claim the gift that you are offering me. Amen

June 16

Jesus, Emmanuel Who Is God With Us, thank you for Rosalyn who said that her most important lesson in life was to live a stress free life by turning it over to God and to stop seeking everybody's approval. May her wisdom guide my life. Amen

June 17

God of Silence, sometimes you are lost to me. I cannot hear you in my heart. I cannot see you in others. I cannot touch you in the garden flowers. I yearn for you but you are silent. I suspect that the problem is me, not you. And yet, still I pray. Undergird me as I seek you. Sustain me as I experience your silence. Amen

June 18

God of Hospitality, you are a welcoming God. You reach out to me with joy and grace. You fill me with your energy. You plant visions in my heart. You embrace me with your wisdom. You guide me with your judgment tempered with love and patience. You are present everywhere I look. You are with me in times of lostness and in times of foundness. Praise be to you! Amen

June 19

Life of All Who Live, I have some suggestions for you:

Take away fear between people of different backgrounds so they can relate.

Eliminate complacency, apathy, and that attitude of "I just don't care."

Add a sense of encouragement for people in hard times.

Lord of all, I like to think that if I had a million dollars, I would:

Provide cars with one year's gas and insurance.

Pay healthcare bills for workers.

Provide scholarships for those who can't go to school any other way.

Provide housing for single fathers.

Provide basic resources for kids whose lack of stability is routine.

But I know that I probably would not be overly generous if I had a million dollars because:

I realize that I stereotype people.

I live in relative comfort.

I experience homeless people on occasion as threats, not people.

(continued)

For some kids instability and lack of basic resources are routine.

So now I beg of you, my maker and defender, help me remember that:

Little things can make a big difference (knowing someone's name, for example).

I can't really help someone until I know her and understand her.

People who live in poverty have so many layers of issues to deal with that it takes strength to get out of the situation.

I can do something…without waiting on that million dollars.

Only through you can everyone experience the world you intend for us—a world of justice, mercy, and peace. Amen

June 20

Loving Jesus, a man told me about how he had planted a gladiolus bulb that his wife brought home from a meeting. She did not know of his act until the first gladiolus bloomed. The next year, even more gladioli appeared. When she was in the hospital before her death, he cut one of those profuse flowers, carried it to her, and both were reminded of hope that grew from one small bulb. Motivate us to be bulb planters even when we personally never reap the harvest. We trust that you will bring forth the first fruits in their season, the time of your choosing. Amen

June 21

Holy Comforter, today a couple of men wiped tears from their eyes because people they care about are dealing with difficult situations. Continue to encourage them to show their strength through their tears. Be with them and with all who empathize with others' pain. Crack through the facades that we protect ourselves with so we can be truly present to those who need us to be with them, through whatever life has next for them. And especially support these two men as they allow their feelings to open their hearts to share your love even in the midst of suffering and fear. Amen

June 22

Protector of All Who Trust, be with people who suffer because they are different. Lead them to people who can celebrate their differences rather than denigrate them. Uplift them with pride in their uniqueness rather than allowing them to be weighed down by it. Help them find others who share some of their outlook or situation so they will know they are not freaks. Surround them with the knowledge that they are your beloved children.

For those of us who distrust people who are different, who put them down because they are unlike us, or who label them with hurtful words, convict us of our judgment and prejudices. Open our eyes to the wonder of your creation, in whatever form it may take. Give us courage to step out with open hearts to embrace those who feel excluded. Help us stand up for those who are not one of the majority.

Jesus our Christ, you died on the cross for all of us. Let us never forget that. Amen

June 23

God of Sabbath, sometimes we get so involved with *doing* that we forget the *being* part. As we move deeper into the summer months, encourage us to contemplate the many ways we can refresh our *being*. Remind us that without healthy *being*, we are lousy *do-ers*. Gently force us to find ways to claim time just for ourselves. Help us remember that as important as all those other people are in our lives, as important as the work is that we devote our days to, as important as our accomplishing things is... our sense of wholeness, deep peace, and inner stability is what gives us the strength for our *doing*.

O God, help us be human beings and not just human do-ers! Amen

June 24

God of the Whirling Planets, the Thrashing Seas, the Purple Mountains, the Rippling Rivers, the Twinkling Stars, the Lilies of the Field, and the Birds of the Air, jolt us out of our apathy so that we notice these wonders. And then once we notice, convince us of our part in protecting and caring for this beauteous and bountiful world we live in. Wake us up. Scare us enough to get our attention. Enliven us to value all the gifts of life that you surround us with. Connect us with others who are impassioned about joining you in caring for this world. We need you to save us from our own indifference. Amen

June 25

Holy God of the Twist and Turns in Life, thank you for whoever created the concept of labyrinths as an aid to spiritual contemplation. I was walking a labyrinth and as I was winding my way out of the center, I noticed that the stones occasionally aligned three straight across. At other times, the three stones did not align at all but still came together as the curves in the path needed them to. I also noticed that in certain sections, the middle stone was rectangular rather than square. Because you had led me to a meditative mood, you helped me notice that this path was much like life. At times everything seems aligned. At other times, things are a little out sync. Sometimes life requires one kind of stone. At other times, another is needed. But the path of life continues.

Thank you for demonstrating that these twists and turns, alignments and disconnections, and even ups and downs exemplify life in general. Sometimes it seems that everything lines up just as it needs to. We have all the resources necessary for the moment.

Everyone is working together joyfully and fully. We are making significant progress toward our goals. At other times, things seem a little off balance. What we've become accustomed to changes. And yet, the changes are important for the path to function as it is intended. Life goes on.

(continued)

Make us aware that all of us, those with adequate resources and those without, are on this path. We have more in common than we have not in common. All of us are connected because we walk the path. Motivate us to celebrate the paths you have given us and help us reach out to each other in our walks. Amen

June 26

God of Justice, because much of contemporary Christianity lacks a fundamental understanding of the essential doctrine of community, we are content to allow homelessness. We ignore the reality that people exist in abandoned and neglected neighborhoods. We can't really say they *live* there because they spend each day trying to just exist.

God of Forgiveness, forgive our apathy and convince us to change. Make us uncomfortable in our isolation from our neighbors whose financial situation is different from ours. Lead us to be in relationship with people in our extended communities. Open our understanding that being apart is hurtful both to us as well as to those we distance ourselves from. Give us a commitment to community. May that intention dwell deep in our souls. Amen

June 27

Holy God, I have a puzzle to share with you. Why is it that some Christians believe that people who are poor are not followers of your way? People who seek financial assistance are often wise and full of witness to the power of your presence and guidance in their lives. Mary said, "I learned to always put God first in my life." Vernard remarked, "God is good. I don't know what the world would be like without him." Adelaide said that she learned "to keep faith and pray. Walk by faith and not by sight."

Maybe William Stringfellow shed enlightenment on this puzzle when he wrote: "Where money is an idol, to be poor is a sin." God of the commandments, help us remove this idol from our altars. Amen

—From

http://www.episcopalcafe.com/thesoul/daily_reading/t he_idolatry_of_money.html web search 10.18.12

June 28

Hip, hip, hooray. I just feel like shouting and praising you, O Wondrous God.

I can sing your praises.

I can dance…when no one is watching.

I can laugh with friends over one of your holy coincidences.

I can shake my hands in joy.

I can tremble with your enlivening energy.

Thank you for this special moment today. Amen

June 29

God of History, yesterday is past, today is now, and the future is unknown. As uplifted as I was yesterday with love for you, today I feel that low. I know that you are not fickle so it must be me.

I promise that I'll remember my overwhelming joy from yesterday and live today moment by moment, always with hope and counting on your promises to be with each of us until the end of time. And yet, my Savior Jesus, you know how well I keep my promises. Sometimes yes and sometimes no. Thank you for being who you are without my needing to be who I cannot be. I trust you in this moment and that's about all I can really commit to today. I hope that's okay. Amen

June 30

God of Vision, when the rain comes steadily, it makes it difficult to see out my office window. I see shapes that I know to be houses but if I did not already know they were houses, I may have no idea of what I am looking at. I suspect that there is a lot in life that I see only as fuzzy or smudged that you wish I could / would see clearly. Assuming that my vision is unfocused because of my own selfishness, self-absorption, and inattentiveness, please clear the film from my eyes so that I can see what you want me to see. I know that seeing means that I can never be the same again. Amen

July 1

God of Mercy, we all make mistakes. Some are accidents that no one could prevent. Some happened because we were careless. Other mistakes occur because we did not prepare, we thought we knew everything already, or we were distracted. We often explain away our mistakes, blame someone for them, or ignore our actions. Push us to accept responsibility for our mistakes. Teach us what we can change. Lead us to seek forgiveness from those we harmed. And always, we ask most sincerely, be merciful with us. Amen

July 2

All Knowing God, thank you for people who give us information when we need it: the grocery store stocker who knows where the special spice is located, the mom who knows how to convince a child to take a nap, and the man who gives directions to the restaurant. Motivate us to never take such kindnesses for granted. Even though technology can give us much information, never let us move away from the power of connecting with others. Amen

July 3

Jesus, Lover of all, there are some people I just cannot love like you ask me to: rude people, whiners, people who are not trustworthy, and pushy people. So what do you expect of me? You really, truly want me to love them? But I don't want to. I don't like them. They aggravate me. What about...just suppose...what if I pray to you each time I encounter one of these folks and ask you to love them while I can't? And will you also help me change my attitude so that maybe...maybe...one day, I can open my heart to them? Amen

July 4

King of Kings, Lord of Lords, today we celebrate the birthday of the United States. It's a day for cookouts, parades, fireworks, and mid-summer parties. It's a day we celebrate being Americans. Remind us of the order of our allegiances, however. You are first, now and always. You and the United States are not the same. Your colors are not just red, white, blue but also orange, black, green, purple, along with many others. Be with us as we party but keep us grounded in you. Remind us that you are a jealous God and our worship belongs to you alone. Amen

July 5

Lord God Almighty, we earnestly ask for your loving oversight and care for all who are engaged in fighting wars they did not create and may not fully understand. We pray for our soldiers. They are being tested in many ways. Undergird them with the sense of their humanity and that of the people they are fighting. Help them realize that those they call the enemy believe in their causes just as our soldiers do. Let our men and women who serve in the military never lose the spark that makes them the people who are loved by their families and friends. When they are in difficult situations, give them wisdom to be strong and calm so they can make the best decision when no option is one they want. Keep them safe but when that is not possible, surround them with loving people to care for them. Hold the families of our soldiers in your tender care as they live with many emotions: fear, pride, loneliness, anger, hope, and love. We ask you to surround them all with your love and mercy. And may we be the answer to the prayers we make. Amen

July 6

God of the Nations, we lift up our leaders. They are charged with making difficult decisions. They are pulled by various interests. They espouse faith in many different ways. Push them to hear your voice in the midst of all the voices that shout for their attention. Give them your wisdom to negotiate challenging issues, especially when the right and just thing to do is not the popular choice.

Fill them with courage to do what is best for all the citizens of the world, not just a special group or limited communities. Strengthen them to be leaders who exhibit your qualities of doing justice, loving mercy, and walking humbly with you. Amen

July 7

God of Hope and Joy, we pray for everyone who works in healthcare: housekeepers, doctors, technicians of all kinds, nurses, nursing assistants, maintenance people, administrators, pharmacists, social workers, chaplains, medical records people, and all the others who help to care for our bodies. We also pray for the all the practitioners of alternative and complementary health practices: craniosacral therapists, massage therapists, acupuncturists, holistic medicine practitioners, and all others who help heal our bodies and our spirits. We pray, too, for those who help care for our emotional and spiritual health: pastoral counselors, psychiatrists, psychologists, licensed counselors and all others who listen and help us process for our good. Help all these people to be instruments of your love and healing. Support them as they themselves struggle with life concerns. Embrace them with the power of your creative energy. Be with each as they serve their fellow human beings. Fill them with patience as they deal with people in pain. Infuse them with the healing touch of Jesus. Amen

July 8

Mighty God, thank you for all the people who enrich our lives: fire fighters, police officers, letter carriers, street maintenance people, garbage collectors, health inspectors, water and sewer workers, government workers, and all those we take for granted until something doesn't work. Then we yell and scream and complain and get angry. Thank you for their commitment to keep us safe and healthy. Remind us of their care of our community. Help us develop sincere appreciation for their work even to the point of putting their lives on the line for us. Help us to see you at work in them. We praise you for the many ways you find to care for us. Amen

July 9

Maker of Light, thank you for all the people who enlighten us: teachers, friends, counselors, artists, writers, ministers, Bible study leaders, support groups, and all the others who walk beside us on our journeys. Thank you for the many ways that you come to us through them by:

Demonstrating small gestures of compassion;

Speaking the most right words at the most right moment;

Offering a slight touch on shoulders;

Confronting lovingly;

Showing old things in new ways;

Turning us around.

You are indeed a God of light. Thank you for guiding our paths. Please stay with us because we are scared of the dark. Amen

July 10

God of the Silent Spaces, sometimes I just need to sit with you and be quiet. Amen

July 11

Holy Spirit, come to me. Speak to me. Let me feel your presence. I need to know that you are here…right now. I cry to you and cannot find you in my inmost being. Where are you? Come, Lord Jesus. Fill me with your love. Open my heart as your dwelling place. Father, I seek you. I yearn for your guidance. Please, please show yourself. Do not hide from me.

I know I will once again know you are here…just not today. Amen

July 12

God of This Day, help me live in *this* day...not yesterday...not tomorrow...but in *this* day. Make me mindful of the details of *this* day. Keep me aware of the signs of your presence *this* day. Touch my heart so I may be present to others *this* day. Let me focus on the things and thoughts that are important *this* day. Thank you for the gift of *this* day. Please help me not to squander it. Amen

July 13

God of Wisdom, Barbara came seeking help and in the process gave us all an invaluable gift. She said, "If you take an opportunity to talk with people around you, there would be far less enemies." Is this one way you meant for us to behave when you instructed us to love our enemies—to love even before we labeled another as "enemy"? Instill in our hearts the commitment to take Barbara's wisdom into our being so that opening ourselves to unexpected relationships will become as natural to us as breathing. Amen

July 14

Why God? Why are people so mean? Why do some get pleasure out of giving brutal pain? Why do people with loads of money believe they have so little? Why do people feel it is their right to take advantage of others before they are taken advantage of themselves? Why do people rape, murder, or kill another's spirit? Why do people ignore another's pain? Why do people simply not care? Why God? What kind of God are you that these kinds of things can happen? Why? Amen

July 15

God of Patience, you truly are an awesome God, allowing us to vent our frustrations and yet loving us still. You continue to reach out to us even when we have built impenetrable walls around our spirit. You nudge us into being able to love again. You gently lead us to worship and praise. You fill us with joy. You feed us nourishment for our visions and dreams. You undergird us with patience and mercy. We will sing songs of praise to you forever…at least until we have our next crisis!!! Amen

July 16

Once upon a time…isn't that the way the story begins? Once upon a time there was a God who people loved and experienced in different ways. To some, this God was a loving parent, a Father or even a Mother. Anyway, this God was the creator and most loving parent. Others experienced this God with a specific name, Jesus. They knew Jesus as a brother, friend, fellow traveler, healer, teacher…and even as the son of God. And still others knew this God as Spirit, closer than their own breath. This Spirit comforted and counseled them. And as this story goes, it turns out that Father, Jesus, and Spirit were all one and the same God.

Thank you, Triune God, for showing your many faces to us so that we can know you as we need to know you at particular times in our lives. Thank you for being the God we trust and for continuing to show us even more aspects of your greatness and awesomeness. Amen

July 17

God of Coincidences, I once heard someone say that coincidences are simply you acting anonymously. Sometimes people describe amazing, unexplainable, serendipitous happenings as *God things*. Thank you for all the ways you intervene in our lives incognito. Help us to recognize more of these God things in our lives. Amen

July 18

Lord of the Dance, sometimes I just want to jump up and shout out loud. I want to whoop it up. I want to twirl and hold my hands in the air. I want to laugh until tears come down. I want to celebrate with abandon.

However, my cultural training makes these things hard for me to do. I treasure my inheritance. Truly I do. Is there a way you can provide me opportunities to let loose praising you without feeling like an idiot? What's that you say? The only thing holding me back from worshiping you with such freedom is me? That I can jump, shout, whoop, twirl, and celebrate with you even if it is in the privacy of my own room? Good idea. Now, how about my feelings of looking weird? Oh, that's my problem? That the weirdness goes away the more I let myself enjoy glorifying you?

Okay, I still will take some convincing but you make a very appealing case, most wonderful God. Hip, hip, hooray! Amen

July 19

God of All, why is it that we define people by one event in their lives? A robber may indeed have done a crime, but he is more than that. He may be a writer or painter. He may be a great humorist. He may be a dedicated friend and family man. He is a thief…but he is more. She may have been a child star and now is a nuclear physicist and a mom. She was a "cute kid" but she is more. A person may be a minister but also a musician, auto mechanic, or skydiver. When we box a person in to a moment of their history without realizing the fullness of his or her humanity, we denounce your creativity in the lives of each of us. We become judges for those we define by their errors and delude ourselves about those we define only by their pinnacle successes.

You have created us in wondrous ways. Keep our minds and hearts open to all people so we can see beyond a single moment and get to know them in 3-d. Amen

July 20

Most Majestic God, when I sit alone in a sanctuary in a church, especially one that has stained glass and high ceilings, I sense your presence in a way I cannot describe. Is it the prisms of light coming through the windows? Is it the height? Is it the silence? Is it the sense of being surrounded by the prayers of hundreds, if not thousands, of worshipers who have sat in the pews throughout the years?

Of course, this is not the only place I feel your communion but there's just something special about being in church. Help me not be lazy and follow the temptation to stay in bed when I can have the opportunity to share this experience with others of faith. Most loving God, thank you for the many ways you let us know that we are not alone. Amen

July 21

God of the In-Between Times, be with those who are unemployed. Help them find meaning in their lives that is not defined by the occupations they have done. Soothe their fears when they become overwhelmed with the financial needs of their families. Give them courage to reach out to others for help when necessary. Encourage their creativity as they redefine what their lives might now be. Hold them close when they believe they cannot go on.

For those who have jobs, open their hearts to reach out to their brothers and sisters. Nudge them not to be tight fisted because of their own fears of the future. Lead all, those employed and those who are not, to find their comfort in the knowledge that you are Lord of the past, present, and future. Help each of us to rely on your guidance, to trust that you will open the right doors, and that we need to care for each other in the in-between times. Amen

July 22

Okay, God, I have a complaint. And I feel so petty making it when people around me have so much more to be concerned about. But sometimes, the things I have to do are just so tedious! They require severe concentration that is exhausting. Or they are so-o-o boring that I want to scream. But the tasks have to be done. Somebody has to do them and sometimes that person is me. I want to find joy in each day but sometimes that just seems impossible when I'm tied up in tedium. Help me find redemption even in the smallest, most irritating tasks. I know that in you, I can find the joy of resurrection living. O God, please may that be so when I'm once again weighed down in details. Amen

July 23

Amazing God, you constantly surprise me. Yesterday, you nudged me to arrive early at a meeting. I decided that I could sit and work on a project while I was waiting. Before I was in my seat for two minutes, you brought a young couple to the meeting early and they sat beside me. You provided me an opportunity to reach out to them in amazing ways. Thank you for your nudges. Help me follow these pushes more consistently. Amen

July 24

God our Father, you know that sometimes parents cannot provide what their children need. I'm not talking about financial needs, even though that may be part of the problem. I'm speaking of those times when a child is burdened by fears, sorrows, hard decisions, or challenges and cannot or will not share those with a parent. Please lift up other adults who can provide wise counsel when parents are excluded at the moment from their child's life. Give parents understanding that they are not at fault when they cannot meet all their child's needs. Help them be grateful for caring adults who help nurture their son or daughter. We need each other. You have created us to be in relationship. Help us to trust in your loving care for parents, their children, and mentoring adults. Amen

July 25

God of Steadfastness and Encouragement, be with people who feel they have no hope. They may be plagued with doubt, discouragement, and disease. They may be bound by past hurts or abuses. They may be overwhelmed with grief. They may be stressed just trying to survive. Bring them your words of hope and encouragement through me or other people, books, movies, music, or television. Let them feel your embrace in the painful hours of the night. Give them strength to hold on until they can begin to breathe your new life in them again. Amen

July 26

God of Peace, Scott Peck has written: "Anyone who believes that world peace won't be established until religious and cultural differences are obliterated...is thereby contributing to the problem rather than the solution. There simply isn't time to do that....The solution lies in the opposite direction: in learning how to appreciate—yea, celebrate—individual cultural and religious differences and how to live with reconciliation in a pluralistic world."

Holy Spirit, help me be a peacemaker. Give me courage to join others in working for peace. Bless me with strength to do what needs to be done to help with reconciliation in our world. Amen

—From

Scott Peck, The Different Drum: Community Making and Peace, Simon and Schuster, Inc. NY, 1987. p 20

July 27

Jesus, I have a question. How is it that you were able to be totally yourself with everyone? You shared your anger when you turned over the tables in the Temple. You showed your tenderness with children. You were frustrated with some of the seeming denseness of your disciples. You were tender when needed; forthright when that was appropriate; chastising when called for. In all the manifestations of your humanity, you were true to yourself and internally honest about who you were. How did you do it?

For us, we act one way with one group of people and change almost totally with another. We assume how honest we can be in one setting and remain guarded elsewhere. We laugh with certain people and find others to be humorless...no matter what. We accept words from one person that—if said by another— would anger us or hurt our feelings. We find it difficult, or even impossible, to be true always to the person you are creating us to be. Infuse us with insight and comfort in being fully human as you desire for us. Amen

July 28

God With Us, Robert T. Standhardt said, "Taking up our cross also means acceptance of what is, often quite against our wills, inflicted upon us. But we take it with openness to the possibility that out of that affliction a blessing can be extracted, by God's grace, and with a little imagination." Help me hold to this wisdom and to live it every day...expectantly and with hope. Amen

—From

http://www.asburyumcarnold.org/userFiles/3058/apri l_15_8am.pdf web search 10.18.12

July 29

God of All Children, for several days now the old gospel song, "Sometimes I Feel Like a Motherless Child" has been reverberating in me. Written in 1899 by William E. Barton, it speaks to the pain of a child born into slavery being ripped from his mother. But today the words seem to reach out to make us think of all those children in our own country who could sing this lament. They are born to poverty and the majority of them will die in poverty. May each of us hear this music deep in our souls and then do something about all children for whom this song speaks truth. Let this old song play over and over until we, as individuals and as communities, decide that no one should ever have to sing this song again. Amen

July 30

God of Wisdom, thank you for people who are willing to share their wisdom when someone asks them a question. They expect nothing in return. They offer insights, counsel, or advice simply because they are natural teachers. They believe in encouraging growth in others and are not threatened that their guidance may help someone outshine them eventually. These people are truly your instruments, Rabbi Jesus. They instruct in your ways, even if they do not profess faith in you. You are able to speak through their hearts of caring and compassion. You truly are a miraculous God. Holy Spirit, come to us through all the gracious people who nurture and mentor us. Amen

July 31

God, Shelter from the Storm, can we just sit together for a while and be quiet? I feel like I'm in the midst of a summer thunderstorm with lightning flashing and thunder clanging like cymbals in a symphony. I need to feel safe and calm while my external world is scary. So I'll sit in this chair and rock to your soothing presence. Thanks. Amen

August 1

Holy God of Radical Change, please let these words of Scott Peck sink deep inside me so they may inform how I live my life.

"We must assume that *genuine* religious belief is radical....If a so-called religious belief is not radical, we must suspect that it is mere superstition, no deeper than the belief that a black cat means bad luck....To put it yet another way, the profession of a religious belief is a lie if it does not significantly determine one's economic, political, and social behavior." Let me live in the truth. Amen

—From

M. Scott Peck, The Different Drum: Community Making and Peace, Simon and Schuster, Inc. NY, 1987, p 246

August 2

Holy God, where are you? I feel disoriented, not focused, and as if my head is spinning. I have no vision for what is next. I wonder if you are even real. Does life have any meaning for any of us? Where is hope? Where is grace? Where is joy? Where are you? Do you even hear my cry? Amen

August 3

Most Mysterious God, you know where I was yesterday. Thank you that my feelings of despair were temporary. But there are some who feel abject lamentation every day, all day. They cannot pray to you because they are very sure you are not there. They truly do not believe in hope, grace, and joy because they have experienced so little in their lives. Help them experience your love by surrounding them with people who can model your way in the manner that best speaks to them. It might be a bartender who listens deeply and offers words of consolation that come from you. It might be a barber or hairdresser who opens the world of your grace to them. It might be a stranger who glows with the light of your love and illumines those dark places in their lives while they wait in line at the grocery store. Come to them in whatever ways and whenever you deem appropriate. If I am to be part of your spirit moving in their lives, give me wisdom, courage, and serenity to reach out. Amen

August 4

Ruler of the Kingdom of Heaven, did John Kenneth Galbraith begin to define some of your kingdom when he defined the good society? His specifications included:

"Employment and an upward chance for all;"

"Reliable economic growth to sustain such employment;"

"Education and...the family support and discipline that serve future participation and reward;"

"Freedom from social disorder at home and abroad;"

"A safety net for those who cannot or do not make it;"

"The opportunity to achieve in accordance with ability and ambition;"

"A ban on forms of financial enrichment that are at cost to others;"

"No frustration of plans for future support and well-being because of inflation;"

(continued)

"A cooperative and compassionate foreign dimension."

I know that *we* cannot create your kingdom on earth but we are partners in your will for our communities. Help us meditate on Galbraith's words and when you want us to act, then push, prod, pull, and encourage us to do our part for your glory. Amen

—From

John Kenneth Galbraith, The Good Society, The Humane Agenda, Houghton Mifflin Co. Boston, 1996, p 31-32

August 5

Holy, Trustworthy God, protect all those who live in danger. They may live with abuse, war, or abject poverty. They may abide in crime ridden communities or in areas plagued by natural disasters. They may be so used to being stressed by fear and the unknown, they do not know what life lived in safety feels like.

Instill in those who are not faced with daily strife the desire and strength to reach out to help those who live with peril as a constant companion. Amen

August 6

God Who Brings Order out of Chaos, thank you for four-way stops. When coming to an intersection with a four-way stop, everyone stops. They look to see if cars are at other corners of the stop. Drivers take turns going through the intersections. They motion other drivers to go ahead of them. They behave better than at traffic lights when they try to make it through the intersection on a yellow light or zoom through without thought to people in other lanes.

Jesus, you taught us to love one another. So thank you for giving us a way to demonstrate that we care for our neighbor when we are in our cars. Keep us safe and mindful of the compassion for and thoughtfulness of our neighbors when we are at four-way stops. Amen

August 7

Spirit of God, today I use the words of George Croly who in 1854 penned:

'Spirit of God, descend upon my heart;

Wean it from earth, through all its pulses move;

Stoop to my weakness, mighty as Thou art;

And make me love Thee as I ought to love." Amen

—From

"Spirit of God, Descend Upon My Heart," The Presbyterian Hymnal, Westminster/John Knox Press: Louisville, KY, 1990, p 326

August 8

God our Maker, thank you for people who are creative, especially those who make beauty out of things others cast off. That's how you work sometimes, isn't it? You create beauty in the lives of people that others have cast off. What a remarkable creator you are. Infuse me with your spirit to be able to see the beauty and possibility of people and things that others see as only trash. Amen

August 9

Holy Spirit, the other day Frank said that "people need help no matter what their situation. These things keep you from shutting down: spirituality, good friends, good personality, a sense of humor, and self-motivation." Open our eyes so we can see past the facades that people wear, faces that hide the negative things that are taking place in their lives. Enable us to be good friends to people in need, to find the small things that can help them get through their trials, and to reach out even when we do not know what to say.

Thank you for Frank and his gentle wisdom that reminds us of how many ways you care for us. Amen

August 10

God of Humanity, a friend gave me figurines of Adam and Eve. Adam fell off the shelf and broke beyond repair. So now there's just Eve. Poor Eve…all alone.

There are Eves who live in our midst. They have lost someone dear to them and all their family is gone. Remind us that loneliness can be a horrible, desolate place to live. Motivate us to find the Eves in our lives so that they will know that life can go on even when Adam is no longer around. Enrich their lives by opening their hearts to others who are available through the activities in their lives. Help us find Eve so that our lives can be made whole as she enriches us with her stories, experiences, and her blossoming forth in your love. Amen

August 11

God our Helper, you sustain me when I am not a very pleasant person to be around. I whine, I complain, I groan, I moan, I fuss, and I am disagreeable. I need your help to live as a person who lives in *your* light, *your* glory, *your* grace, and *your* mystery. Be patient with me, help me, and sustain me as I learn daily to be your faithful disciple. Amen

August 12

God of Peace, a long time ago I received this prayer from an unknown source. It is my prayer today:

Lead us from dying to living;

From illusion to truth;

Lead us from despair to hope.

Lead us from hatred and unlove;

Through forgiveness and reconciliation;

To cooperation and peace.

May love and peace fill ourselves, our neighbor, the world, our universe. Amen

August 13

Jesus, Redeemer, thank you for healed relationships, improved communication, and openness to listening. Painful situations, long held estrangements, and deep hurts can seem impossible to overcome. And yet, miracles do happen and closed hearts open. Thank you for infusing your healing powers into relationships that seemed damaged beyond repair. Amen

August 14

God of Questions and Answers, I heard that there are three great questions that make us human. They are:

    1. What is really real?

    2. Who am I?

    3. What is life all about?

I cannot answer these questions without you in my life, thoughts, heart, and spirit. Please dwell within me as I seek answers now and for all my days. Amen

August 15

Jesus Christ, Logos, Word of God, I was thinking about how wonderful the alphabet is. With twenty-six letters, we can create thousands, maybe even millions of words. Depending on how we order the letters, we can use them for evil or for good. We can hurt or we can heal. We can destroy or build up. The letters are really very simple but can be used in such complex ways. Let us always use the alphabet to further your kingdom. Thank you for A-B-C-D-E-F-G-H-I-J-K-L-M-N-O-P-Q-R-S-T-U-V-W-X-Y-Z. Amen

August 16

God of All Our Days, summer is beginning to wind down. People are thinking about school's beginning. Others are remembering their vacations or still wishing they could take one. Some complain about the weather. It is a time of year that feels like being between one thing and another. When those times of life occur, help us to be especially mindful of listening to your voice, heeding your guidance, and being patient in a time of waiting. Fill us with hope that as one door closes another is opening. We depend on your glorious involvement in our lives. Help us never to take your care for granted and to respond as your true disciples. Amen

August 17

Holy God, I like those little icons at the top of my computer screen. I can make things happen with just the click of a mouse. I even have options with some of them. I click and more things appear that I can do. I'd like life to have icons. I could press a button and what I wanted to happen would.

But sometimes, I want to do something with my computer and I cannot find the icon or option list to allow me to do what I want. Sometimes life is like that as well. The answer or solution is hidden. I don't know the right question to ask. I don't understand enough about the computer functions to make it do what I want.

I guess I approach you sometimes as an icon. I want you to act when I push a button. I want a solution and amazingly one appears. However, I don't understand at other times. I seek something that is not currently possible or I just get frustrated that you don't give me an icon! Forgive me for trying to use you like I use the icons. And always help me remember that you are with me, even when I don't seem to know how to reach out to you. Amen

August 18

God Who is Perfect Love, thank you for all the people who love me in so many different ways. Some love me for who I am as a professional, others love me as a parent, daughter, or grandparent. People love me as a friend or a church colleague. People love me when we happen to see each other at work or out shopping. They don't all love me the same and they certainly don't all express their love. But they support me in ways even unknown to them. They surround me with positive expressions of energy, vision, and joy. They pray for me, laugh with me, cry with me, and just spend time with me. Some I see regularly, some are only in my thoughts, and others keep contact through technology. Occasionally even a stranger smiles and fills me with love. All of this love begins and ends with you. Thank you. Amen

August 19

God of Health and Wholeness, I pray for people waiting for organ transplants. Strengthen them in their sickness while they hope for the gift of life. I pray also for those who donate organs. For those donors who are alive and share, continue to enrich their generous spirits. Thank you for their sacrifices of love that truly enable someone to live with quality. For those families who choose to give organs from dearly loved family members who lost their lives, comfort them in their grief and console them with the wonder of their generosity.

Thank you for medical professionals who are able to take organs from one person and give them to others. Continue to guide their hands and minds as they perform unbelievable miracles within your care and guidance. For all those waiting and for those donating, undergird each with your grace and knowledge that they are held dearly in your love. Amen

August 20

Jesus, Healer, be with those who await diagnoses for medical conditions. Not knowing or having to endure test after test without clear results erodes their enjoyment of life. Give them answers so that they can begin treatments or breathe sighs of relief. Help them have confidence that you are with them as they wait, when they receive their diagnosis, and during treatment—whatever it may be.

Lord, also be with those family members and friends who wait with them—in fear, with love, in hope, and with fatigue. May they be undergirded by your love so that they will know they are not alone. Give them courage to walk with their loved one when the answers are those hoped for and especially when they are not.

For those of us who watch the waiting, give us wisdom to know how to support people we care about. Make us mindful of the tiny things we might be able to do to help: listen, care for a child, clean a house, cook a meal, do laundry, drive to an appointment, pick up toilet paper, or walk a dog. Above all, open our eyes to the promise that you are with all of us still to the end of the age. Amen

August 21

Father God, you know that sometimes your children are just rebellious. So we hope you understand that parents need help when their own children are rebellious and hard-headed. You know the pain of watching a child make a decision for his or her life that seems totally wrong. Holy Spirit, infuse parents with patience, give them the power of prayer, and fill them with assurance that you are a resurrection God. You can bring life even in the midst of death. You can bring dry bones to life. You are with them...and their children...even when your presence may not be evident.

We ask that you move into the hearts of children who are struggling to grow up and become adults. Find ways to speak so they can hear. Give them courage to move against the pressure of their peers. Plant wisdom in their spirits so they can become the people you intend them to be.

We know you understand about the challenges of dealing with rebellious children. We depend on you to get us all through this. Amen

August 22

God of Abundance, we pray for people who do not have adequate resources to pay their bills. They live in constant stress laced with fear. Open the hearts and wallets of people who are able to help with the immediate situation.

More importantly, God of power and might, unseal the mouths of people who can ask the questions about what is wrong with our community and government systems that people are forced to choose between medications and heat, food and rent, or transportation and clothing. Open the hearts of decision makers who can address the systems, powers, and principalities that create environments that force people to ask others for utility money.

You are a God of miracles. Help bring miracles to the lives of people in need, advocates who ask tough questions, or power people who can change the systems. We need you NOW. Amen

August 23

Holy Jesus, how in the world could you let this happen? How is it that kids could decide to practice their boxing moves by stringing up a baby to use as a punching bag? How could you let a woman be raped as she took her morning run? How could you allow a homeless guy to be murdered just for a cigarette? How? Just answer me.

As with Job, I say that my ways are not your ways. Still, occasionally, sometimes, it would be nice to understand the evil in this world. But maybe not. That might be too frightening indeed. So my prayer is for you to touch the hearts of every person who lives on this earth so that your will may be done in every situation, in every place, and in every time. Amen

August 24

Most Merciful God, thank you for allowing our bodies to hurt. When my right shoulder begins hurting, I know that I've been on the computer too long and need to take a break. When my knee hurts, I know that I've been wearing "cute" shoes too frequently and need to go back to ones that protect my feet. When my head hurts, I know that I probably need to rest. When my back hurts, I know that I've been trying to overdo. These hurts are built-in signals that I am not taking care of this body that you gave me. Thank you for the warning signs. Help me not ignore them. I'd also like you to make me aware when I am pushing hard on things that are not particularly important so that I won't begin hurting in the first place. Please help me discern what is important and what is urgent. Amen

August 25

God of the Saints, St. Augustine said that love looked like this: "It has hands to help others. It has the feet to hasten to the poor and needy. It has eyes to see misery and want. It has ears to hear the sighs and sorrows of God's children. This is what love looks like."

O God, never let me shirk the requirements of love. Amen

—From

www.brainyquote.com/quotes/quotes/s/saintaugus148 553.html. Web search 8.2.14

August 26

God of Joy, some people try to demean others by calling them silly. I assume they mean that they think the person has little sense or is absurd. But the first definition of silly in Webster's Dictionary is that silly is "simple; plain; or innocent." Let us be silly when it comes to proclaiming our faith in you. Love for you and your love for us is simple...and oh, so complex. You love us as we are—that's simple—and complex. You love us without ostentation, in other words plainly. We don't need to "put on airs" for your love. And you declare our innocence when we recognize our need for your mercy and forgiveness. So can we be silly together? Can we love you and others simply, plainly, and innocently? What an amazing quality of love—to be silly! Amen

—From

David B. Guralnik, Editor in Chief, Webster's NewWorld Dictionary, Second College Edition, Simon and Schuster: New York, NY, 1984, p 1326

August 27

Holy God, is prayer more for me or for you? Does it really matter as long as I keep praying? The important thing is for me to thank you, praise you, lift up my needs and those of others, and keep reminding myself to stay in touch. I know that's enough—that you want me to stay in relationship with you and other people. So my question doesn't really matter. I'll just keep praying even when I'm not sure what or why I'm doing it. Amen

August 28

Holy Spirit, in this hurry up world, help us to slow down. Do we think that we are you, God? Do we believe we have to accomplish things that only a magician could do? Do we believe that the more we do the worthier we are? Do we want our children to never have time to enjoy being a kid, full of wonder and imagination? Do we really trust that we are in control of our lives as long as we keep running on the treadmill of life? Why do we hurry so when there is so much to enjoy when we reduce our pace. We enjoy better health, we notice wild flowers, we see our children relax into happy people we want to hold close, and our faith deepens. Holy Lord, help us slow down to the pace that you have set for us. Amen

August 29

Dearest Lord Jesus, I have a confession to make. I don't like to be around people who are chipper. I know that some people just have an exuberant personality and I am okay with them. I'm talking about the people who put on "chipper-ness" when they believe it is to their advantage, they think it is appropriate for the occasion, or they are trying to win me or others over to their agendas.

Okay, I'm listening. You want me to remember that "chipper-ness" may be covering a deep-seated sense of hurt or inadequacy? Or that false exuberance may be how they learned to survive as a child? Or they simply like putting on different roles in life as the mood strikes them? And you want me to remember that you love them as your child just as you love me? I hear you but I'm going to need your help. So I pray that you give me patience with "chipper-ness" and that I relate to the person underneath with grace, love, and joy. Is that about right? O Lord, forgive me my judgmental thoughts and be with me in this growth area for me. Amen

August 30

Loving God Who Surrounds Us All with Your Care, today my prayer is a traditional Gaelic prayer:

> God to enfold me,
>
> God to surround me,
>
> God in my speaking,
>
> God in my thinking,
>
> God in my sleeping,
>
> God in my waking,
>
> God in my watching,
>
> God in my hoping. Amen

—From

Carmina Gadelica and collected by Lois Rock in Celtic Prayers to Guard and Guide You, Good Books, PA, 2001, p 10)

August 31

Jesus, Son of God, Savior of the World, Allison Adkins once wrote, "We are not called to fix people, but we are called to love them while they are trying to fix themselves." Help me remember that you are the Messiah, not me. Instill in me the acceptance that I cannot change anyone. I certainly cannot fix people much as I might try or even want to. Infuse your love for them into me. Encourage me to pray for them as they grow under your care in their own way at their own pace with their own mistakes. Amen

—From

Allison Adkins, Editor, South Carolina United Methodist Advocate, April 1996

September 1

Holy God, give me patience and fortitude. The devices that are designed to help me do my work are totally and completely aggravating today. It seems that none of the machines that I depend on are working properly for me. I'm really frustrated. So what is your lesson for me in all this?

Ah-h-h. Does any of this have to be done today? Will there be significant consequences if the work takes several days to complete? Am I putting demands on myself that no one else is? Am I forgetting that life in you is not always smooth and sometimes I ignore the important things you place in my life and pay attention to things that really do not matter? Help me prioritize by what is important in your kingdom. Give me patience while I work on letting go of the frustrations while I'm still learning from you. Amen

September 2

Giver of Good Gifts, thank you for pets. They enrich our lives with their companionship. They make us relate to them even when we want to ignore the world and everything that is in it. They remind us that life is not perfect when we must clean up after them. They bring us joy with their loyalty and grief with their deaths.

Lord Jesus, did you have a pet? Probably not with all your travels. If not, you missed out on one of the pleasures that human beings can experience. So thank you for allowing us the opportunity to love your creatures and to experience their connections with us. Amen.

September 3

God of All Creation, I want to talk with you today about magnolia trees. They symbolize to me how living life in your way can be. Sometimes, as in the summer, they produce saucer-size, beautiful white flowers that smell sweet and make life rich with their fragrance. Life with you is sometimes that heady with sensory delights.

In the spring, however, magnolia trees drop their old leaves…lots of leaves. But that is what we need to do in our kingdom lives—to let go of the old ways to create space for the new.

In the fall, they drop their seed pods that hurt when they fall on my head. Small boys use them as grenades in their play. The pods are aggravating to remove from the yard but they must be cleaned up so no one will turn an ankle while walking in the garden. Sometimes you have to take drastic measures to get our attention. Just as the seed pods produce new trees, the "grenades" you allow in our paths—illness, grief, challenges, and frustrations—can create new life for us.

In the winter, the tree remains green reminding us of your everlasting love for us. The tree at all times provides shelter for birds, shade for yards, and leaves that filter our air.

(continued)

Thank you for magnolia trees with all their gifts for us. Help us always to be reminded of your love when we're raking those leaves or picking those pods. Remind us that lives of faith are multi-dimensional— just like living with a magnolia tree is. Amen

September 4

God of Mercy,

When I complain about people tracking dirt into my house, help me be grateful that I have a house.

When I get stuck in traffic, help me use the time to meditate with you about the good things of my life.

When people disappoint me, help me see their own disappointments in life and be gracious.

When someone tries to make me do something, give me insight into my proper response for that particular situation.

When I want an item, help me wait to allow the desire to lessen if that is what needs to be.

When I am confused, give me people to help me sort out my confusion.

Most Merciful God, you are as close as my own breath and as vast as the universe and beyond. Keep me on track as I strive to live the life you're creating in me. Amen

September 5

God Who Speaks in the Stillness of the Night, open my ears so I can hear your voice. Give me calm to pay attention. Uphold me when I am anxious in the dimness of my thoughts. Be with me when I fear my next steps…if I know that they are.

Holy Spirit, feed my spirit, be my comforter, stand up as my advocate, and be merciful with me when I am dense about all this. Amen

September 6

God of All Ages, thank you for elderly people who demonstrate to younger folks how to age gracefully...

People who are full of joy even with physical limitations;

People who celebrate more than complain;

People who reach out to others even after significant losses in their own lives;

People who willingly share their wisdom and time with others;

People who choose to live well all their days;

People, who because of their deep faith and joy for their future, teach others how to die.

Thank you for this powerful witness of aged wisdom.

Amen

September 7

Holy of Holies, thank you for those coincidences that remind me that you are ever present in my life:

When someone happens to drop in with helpful assistance at a time I'm about to pull out all my hair;

When an acquaintance sends a thinking-of-you e-mail...for no reason;

When a waitress gives me—for no apparent reason—an extra glass of tea that I then give to a homeless man who approaches me when I leave the restaurant;

When seemingly insignificant incidences happen at the very moment that makes them significant.

Most loving God, you surely do know how to love us. Do you think we'll ever figure out how to love as you love? Amen

September 8

Lord Jesus, Howard Friend wrote: "I am gradually learning to ground all my interactions in the philosophical, theological, and psychological assumption that even the person I view as a most repulsive and offensive adversary holds a part of the truth...a truth which I need to make my own truth more whole." Is this part of loving our enemies—to learn from them what they have to teach? Is this part of being a peacemaker — to acknowledge that everyone/anyone has something powerful to offer to the responsibility of living? Help this lesson to establish deep roots in those who choose to follow you. Amen

—From

Howard Friend, "Holding the Center," The Other Side, July-August, 1996

September 9

Holy Comforter, be with people who have to hear bad news: lay-offs, medical diagnoses, family troubles, or community problems. Comfort them in their anxiety, give them hope that they will survive the pain, and instill in them resolve to discover and take positive steps even in the midst of their trauma. When the issues involve those they love, give them strength to be comforters, advocates, and supporters. When the issue is theirs, lead them to people who can help them get through the initial stages of shock and move toward ideas for coping.

For those of us who learn of others' situations, give us wisdom to know appropriate ways to reach out, words that speak to their hearts, and motivation to help them overcome when possible. Some of our neighbors are in pain. Lead us to love them as you would have us love. Amen

September 10

Steadfast and Loving God, thank you for those sticky roller things that remove lint and dog hair and stuff from clothing. Using them enables us to look clean and neat. Is there any chance that we could have such a roller to remove the sins from our own lives so that we could be clean and neat?

No? Why? Oh, that's what Jesus took care of already. I get it but sometimes, I don't really get it. I still could use one of those rollers. Work with me, okay? Amen

September 11

God Who Sustains Us, this date will forever remind those of us who live in the United States of the fear and horror of the hijacked planes and the Twin Towers, the Pentagon, and the field in Pennsylvania. On that day, fires of compassion for people who suffer around the world were ignited. On that day, flames of hatred for those who are not like us were lit. On that day, the horrors of what religious fervor can do were rekindled. Decisions—both heroic and disastrous—were made this day. We live with these dual legacies. Help us to remember always this date and to use it as a catalyst for peacemaking and not violence. Be with us even in the midst of terror so that we can hear *your* voice rather than the tumult of the mob. We need your grace, guidance, and wisdom so that we do not make religion a weapon rather than a way of love. Amen

September 12

Radiant and Glorious God, your love is found true by many people because of the warmth and guidance they experience in their lives. Your love is also found true when it is laced within discipline or judgment. Love is shallow without you confronting those places in our lives that are hurtful, sinful, or damaging to ourselves or others. Love is cheap without you pushing us to face ourselves in all our dimensions—those we appreciate as well as those we detest. Love is not love but apathy or even anarchy without calling the powers and principalities to responsibility for their damaging and hateful acts. We like thinking of the warm feelings of your love. We resist accepting the harsh judgments and corrections of your love. Help us to know that every moment of our lives is within your grace so we can be the persons you are creating us to be. Give us vision. Amen

September 13

Watchful and Caring God, when people are homeless, hungry, abused, victims of war, and abandoned, some of us wonder if you really are paying attention.

Oh…you are. You are bringing homeless, hungry, abused, victims of war, and abandoned people to our attention. You are making sure that some of us see some of them. You are not letting them go unnoticed. And because of that, you want us to do something. You are choosing to work through us. You are using us to watch and care.

We confess we are not doing a very good job. Please forgive us, motivate us to get involved, and give us courage and strength to be about your work in our world. Amen

September 14

Source of Peace, today I pray for people who in the past have caused me pain. Most of them did not intentionally mean to hurt me. They just said something that stabbed me deeply. Many were working from their own damaged places and I was simply the unlucky target. Help me release all of them to you so you can surround them with your loving light. If they are still held hostage by places of damage, heal them and give them serenity and peace.

Where I have caused pain to others, forgive me. Show me when and if there are ways to improve situations. Open doors for setting things right when the damage has been mutual. Help us wounded people find ways to move beyond past damage and experience blessings of release. When that is not possible, surround both those who caused the hurt and those who received the hurt with your love so each can let pain caused by the other go to you for your understanding and compassion. Amen

September 15

Friend of the Stranger, open our minds and hearts to the strangers in our midst, especially those people who have left their homelands. They have come here for many reasons: opportunity, escape, family, or education. But all of them are placed in situations where the familiar is absent and the new is strange or frightening. They are challenged by learning another language, eating new foods, and experiencing new customs. Sometimes they experience resentment, insults, and fear from their neighbors in their new country. Be with them so they know that they are not alone. Just as you traveled with Abraham and Sarah, guide them on their journeys.

May those of us for whom this country has been home for a long time be understanding, welcoming, and hospitable. Let us remember the words of the writer of the book of Hebrews: "Do not neglect to show hospitality to strangers, for by doing that some have entertained angels without knowing it." Amen

—*From*

Hebrews 13:2

September 16

God of No Boundaries, Joseph Fort Newton has said, "People are lonely because they build walls instead of bridges." Create in us a bridge building mentality and will. Amen

—From

http://quotationsbook.com/quote/24252/

web search 10.23.12

September 17

God of Justice, I pray for people who experience the world as unfair—and who among us has not? When people believe they have been treated unjustly, give them a safe place to vent their anger so that they do not cause harm to themselves or others. When they have had time to process what happened, help them claim their real and valued feelings while considering their own part in whatever happened. If they acknowledge that some of what happened was because of something they did, help them learn from their lessons and be gentle with themselves in their growing process. If they indeed were treated totally unfairly, plant seeds of forgiveness in their hearts, give them safe people to talk through their situation with, and help them move beyond the hurtful experience.

Because you are a God of justice, revenge or retribution does not belong to them or us. Help us trust in your providence and claim our part in forgiving. Amen

September 18

Most Loving Creator, Redeemer, and Sustainer, thank you for those people in our lives who love us unconditionally. Even though they are few in number, they witness powerfully to the awesomeness of your love for each of us. Thank you for these people of profound blessings. Amen

September 19

Searcher of Hearts, today I need to be silent and listen for your word in my heart. Amen

September 20

Strength of the Weak, sometimes I become afraid that people will criticize something that I've written in my prayers to you. I fear they will judge me or my understanding of Divinity-You: Father, Son, Holy Ghost; Creator, Redeemer, Sustainer; Jesus, Christ, Lord, and all the other names I use to address you. Take away my fear so that I will continue to share our communications with others. If these words help someone grow in faith, thank you for that. Do not let me get in the way of a person finding faith in you. Do not let me be a stumbling block to their deepening faith in your grace, hope, and love. Give me words that show forth your love and grace. Amen

September 21

Holy God of the Sabbath, thank you for weekends. They offer time to switch from one way of being to another. The regimen of the clock can be set aside for a brief time. Thinking about responsibility of the work place can move to thinking more about family, home, play, and friends. However, some people do not welcome weekends.

Some have no work to break from.

Some are alone with no one who cares for them.

Some have no faith to support and guide them.

Some work day and night, seven days a week and find no rest.

Even as you hold these, our neighbors, in your love, help us to make your grace and compassion tangible for them. Make us aware of their plight. Lead us to discover ways to open their worlds so that weekends become a joy and not a drudge for them. Amen

September 22

God of Love, thank you for people who model the joy and nurture of long, happy marriages. In our time, marriages that last forty, fifty, or even sixty years are rare. Couples are bombarded by things that are serious as well as things that are trivial. Illness and death interfere with long-term marriages. Anger, breaking trust, economic woes, and disillusion destroy commitments. So when people have wrinkles and creaking joints and still look with soft eyes at each other, hold hands when they walk, and kiss before one of them leaves on an errand, we witness the amazing power of love. We see a glimpse of what living daily in your love looks like. We are moved by steadfastness—a term readily applied to you. Thank you for this witness. Amen

September 23

Has being human always been hard? Sometimes I roll along without a care in the world and at other times I'm plagued with fear, doubt, anxiety, apathy, and fatigue. At times I want to live forever and at others, that's the scariest thought I can have. Some people seem calm and serene all the time. Are they really? Some people seem angry all the time? Really?

Incarnate God, Jesus Christ, you know what I'm talking about. You've been here. Did you sometimes wonder what in God's name being human was all about? And yet, you did it. You showed us about love, healing, prayer, hope, forgiveness, and walking even toward torture and death. You taught us about joy and eating with friends. You showed us that reaching out to people who were not "acceptable" could enrich our lives beyond measure. You know the challenges and delight in being human. Help me live more in the delight side of humanity. I could do with fewer challenges right now.

Oh...oh...so you know about my challenges? And...and...you're here with me while I take this particular walk? In the delights and the challenges you are here? Oh my, thank you my God, my Christ, my brother, my friend, my advocate, and my hope. Amen

September 24

God of the Birds of the Air, thank you for birds. Some of them are showy with their flashy colors and riotous squawks. Some are tiny and precious in their compactness. Some are aggravating with their, shall we say, evidences of bodily functions in places we'd rather not see! Some sing beautifully so that they gladden our spirits. Some are aggressive in protecting their territory and little ones; some are reclusive and delight us when we catch a glimpse of them. Some are colorful while some are drab. Some are big and some are small. Some like living near us humans and some want only the open field or the deep jungle.

Birds remind us of the vastness and variety of your creation. Because you care for each of them, we are overwhelmed with the possibility of that kind of love and care for each of us. When we see a bird hopping on the ground, walking across grass, sitting in a tree, or soaring in the air, remind us to offer up a prayer of gratitude to you for your love and your creation. Amen

September 25

God of the Universe, I can see my house on the computer because of satellite photos of my neighborhood. But no matter how hard I look, I cannot see me or my family or my friends or anyone who lives in my community. From the satellite photo, we are all invisible. But not from you. Amazing! Amen

September 26

Creator, you know about to-do lists. When are they part of your plan for our lives and when are they *our* plan for our lives? How do we discern? I'll put you on my to-do list so we can have time to discern which is which. Amen

September 27

Jesus, sometimes the only prayer that needs to be prayed is the one you taught: "Our Father, who art in heaven, hallowed by thy name. Thy kingdom come, thy will be done on earth as it is in heaven. Give us this day our daily bread; and forgive us our sins as we forgive those who sin against us. And lead us not into temptation, but deliver us from evil. For thine is the kingdom and the power and the glory, forever." Amen

September 28

God of the Universe, thank you for the sixty-four colors in the crayon box and for all the other colors of this world. As kids we were excited to see the pristine line up of points of different hues when we reverently opened a new container. Possibilities abounded for what those colors could offer in our lives.

Lover of All Humanity, help us be as excited when we encounter the many hues of humanity. Rather than noticing and magnifying our differences, lead us to find our commonalities, our similarities, and our connections. In your loving ways, demonstrate how we all live together in the same box. Highlight how our colors are intensified and made more beautiful when we stand tall, side by side. We delight in praising you for creating us in so many wondrous ways. Amen

September 29

You know what, God? Sometimes being loving is just not that appealing. I don't want to see you in my neighbors. I don't want to listen attentively or compassionately. And I really don't want to turn the other cheek. I'd rather complain, accuse, ignore, and glare. I'd be content to sit in my self-made world and glow in my self-righteousness. So there, I've said it!

So now, what are you going to do about it? Nothing? You mean you're going to allow me to continue on this path? You're not going to make me love anybody? It's my decision? Oh, well, then...maybe after a day or two, I'll reconsider my position. Okay? Thanks. Amen

September 30

Holy God, Ruler of All Nations, I pray for leaders around the world. I suspect that some of them confuse serving your people wisely and gracefully with serving themselves, their ambitions, and greed. Intervene in their lives so they can reflect your thoughts and desires rather than their own. Temper their power with compassion so they can bring peace and fairness to all who live and die under their leadership. Soften their hearts to see the most vulnerable among us so they may build real strength in all their followers. Help them grasp the phenomenal reality that violence only breeds violence until there are none of us left.

God of Peace, without your promise of saving the world, we would be hopeless as we read the news and listen to the commentaries. We call on your loving kindness and seek to find our part in your desires for this world. We depend on your power, your love, and your mercy. Amen

October 1

Holy God, your apostle Paul taught that "the members of the body that seem to be weaker are indispensable, and those members of the body that we think less honorable we clothe with greater honor, and our less respectable members are treated with greater respect; whereas our more respectable members do not need this. But God has so arranged the body, giving the greater honor to the inferior member, that there may be no dissension within the body, but the members may have the same care for one another. If one member suffers, all suffer together with it; if one member is honored, all rejoice together with it."

May I absorb these words into my deepest self so I may live them to your honor and glory. Amen

—From
I Cor. 12: 22-26

October 2

Holy God of the Entire World, give me patience to wait to see the truth of what is in front of me. Give me sight to see brothers and sisters rather than monsters and strangers. Open my heart, mind, and vision to experience the wonder of your creation in all its variety. Amen

October 3

Father, Son, and Holy Spirit, thank you for the gift of your triune being. Even though I may not understand the theological concept of it—scholars, philosophers, and theologians have argued about it for centuries—I understand the profound value of relationship that is inherent in you. Open me to sharing that kind of deep connection with you and with everyone I meet. By living in relationship, I experience your amazing love, joy, and grace. Amen

October 4

God of All Good Gifts, thank you for erasers. They are so handy when I need to get rid of something: a stray mark on the wall, mistakes on a paper, cancelled meetings in my calendar, and wrong words in a cross word puzzle. Wouldn't it be lovely to have an eraser to get rid of all those things I'd like to forget, dismiss, or ignore in my life? I know that I can come to you and claim your forgiveness for my mistakes and my sins but that does not mean that I'm excused from making amends, seeking resolution, or admitting my error to the person I wronged. Help me to take up my eraser when it comes to setting things right and cleaning up my mess. Amen

October 5

God who challenges us to grow as your disciples, this day my prayer is one known as the Franciscan Benediction:

"May God bless us with discomfort at easy answers, half-truths, and superficial relationships, so that we may live deep within our hearts.

"May God bless us with anger at injustice, oppression, and exploitation of people so that we may work for justice, freedom, and peace.

"May God bless us with tears to shed for those who suffer from pain, rejection, starvation and war, so that we may reach out our hands to comfort them and turn their pain into joy.

"And may God bless us with enough foolishness to believe that we can make a difference in this world, so that we can do what others claim cannot be done."

God of discipline and judgment, make this blessing my own. Amen

—From

http://epistle.us/inspiration/franciscanbenediction.ht ml web search 10.24.12

October 6

"A Cherokee elder, a tribal story goes, sat with his grandchildren around a roaring fire, teaching them about life. 'There's a terrible fight between two wolves going in inside me,' he began, his eyes glistening, reflecting the flames, the children's eyes widening. 'One represents fear, anger, envy, sorrow, and resentment.' He went on. 'And the other stands for joy, peace, love, hope, and kindness.' He paused and the children leaned forward, resting their hands on their palms. One inquisitive youngster asked, 'Grandfather, who will win?' The old man looked into each child's eyes before he answered, 'The one I feed.'"

O God, helper of the weak, give me strength to nourish in others joy, peace, love, hope, and kindness so I may honor and praise you. I cannot be strong without your help. I depend on you. Amen

—*From*

Howard E. Friend, Jr., Gifts of an Uncommon Life, The Alban Institute: Herndon, VA, 2008, p. 149

October 7

Source of All Blessing, help us be the answer to the prayers we make.

When someone needs to be understood, let us be that understanding.

When someone seeks a place to soar, let us encourage their flying.

When someone yearns for a place to ask questions, let us create the space for answers to shimmer.

When someone requires somewhere for their feelings to be heard, let us be that place.

When someone desires to be accepted, let us be that openness.

When someone hopes for a place to grow and thrive, let us fulfill that hope.

We want to live as you want us to live. We want to demonstrate to the world the kind of God we worship and serve. We ask for you to enable us to be a blessing in your name to others. Amen

—From

Adaptation by Beth Lindsay Templeton of a poem by William Crockett, "A People Place"

http://www.culham.ac.uk/sg/weekend/poem.pdf   web search 12.04.2012

October 8

God of Forgiveness, I need some of that... forgiveness.

I confess that people irritate me with their constant requests, whining, and demands.

I confess that I really like having more clothes than I can wear in a month.

I confess that I take for granted the privileges my skin color provides.

I confess that I don't want to feel the suffering other people must endure.

I confess that I like being blind to the needs of other people.

I confess that I ignore the demands of my body and health.

I confess that I don't even want to list all the things I need to confess.

Please forgive me and change my heart so that I can turn around those things I just confessed. Amen

October 9

God, Giver of Life and Health, we thank you for the people who work at free medical clinics and for their witness that healing is one of your many miracles to us. We thank you for their skills in medical services and in personal caring that mean the difference between suffering and wholeness. We thank you for the financial gifts that underwrite the services offered around our state. Gracious God of Hope and Joy, we pray that all of us will be inspired by your compassion so that we, too, may be instruments of healing and the building up of people. Amen

October 10

Source of Strength, it's one of those days. I just don't think I can make it. I've run out of vision, energy, compassion, and interest in anything. I'm just going to give myself a mental health day today, knowing that you are beside me. I know that I will once again claim the strength that you instill in me but just for today, I'm pulling the covers over my head and disappearing. Amen

October 11

Source of All True Joy, bubble up in our world. We hear so much that is negative, hateful, mean, and violent. Bring joy in all its forms to us so that we can engage and overcome the damaging parts of life. Your joy is our hope embodied in your son Jesus and is grounded in love, grace, peace, and faith. We need your joy and your hope. We count on your steadfast promises for new life. So bubble up, please? Amen

October 12

God of All Times and Places, today is the date our country remembers the discovery of North America by Christopher Columbus. This day reminds us that what is a celebration for some of us is a travesty for others. Our brothers and sisters who were already on this continent when Columbus arrived may have wondered where you were as they lost more and more of their land and their ways.

God of Hidden Answers, alert us to the many ways that our good intentions hurt some people while helping others. Open our minds to look for ways to reduce the unintentional harm we cause even when we believe that we are aligned with your calls to justice. Reduce our pride in our accomplishments so that we can be wise to the gaps in our awareness. We want to be your good servants. Sustain us when we fall short and forgive our arrogance in our successes. Amen

October 13

God of All Life, I just learned that the word "lifestyle" was not even in most dictionaries in the early 1970s. Now I hear about lifestyles all the time. Does this indicate how our priorities have changed? How would homeless people define "lifestyle"?

God of Holy Wonder, make me look into your face on the cross. Help me hold this image as a kind of mirror to my face when I focus my efforts on my lifestyle. Shine your light on people whom I find inconvenient: those who are homeless, mentally ill, addicted, lazy, or manipulative. Help me contrast my "lifestyle" with theirs. Break open my resistance to change how *I* live so they may have opportunity to change how *they* live. Without you, I am lost in my own definition of lifestyle. Let this not be so. Amen

October 14

God of Holy Timing, give me patience...

When technology doesn't work as it is supposed to, help me remember that many people in our world do not have access to computers, electricity, phones, and other *conveniences*.

When people do not do what I expect, help me remember that I am not the focus of their world.

When someone expects me to do what they want right now, help me remember that they are as frantic about getting things done as I am.

When life seems out of balance, show me those who would love to have *only* the problems that I struggle with.

When I am confused about another's reaction, help me embrace him/her with all the love and compassion I can muster.

Loving God, I can't do this without you. Be patient with me as you help me develop patience. Thanks. Amen

October 15

Lover of the World, thank you for all those people who enhance our community's beauty:

Sanitation workers who haul away our garbage;

Lawn maintenance people who keep our public spaces neat and pretty;

House painters who keep our homes attractive;

Artists who inspire us with their creativity;

People who pick up dead animals.

Without these dedicated individuals, our lives would be mired in ugliness, filth, and disease. Keep us mindful of their significant contributions to our lives and open us to ways to show our appreciation of their service. We know you value every person and every gift. Prod us to do the same. Amen

October 16

O God of Creation, we praise you for the vast details in our bodies that you designed:

Eyelashes that keep dust and trash out of our eyes;

Bladders that dump our body's waste;

Tongues that function for eating, speaking, and licking ice cream cones;

Big toes that help us balance;

Tonsils that keep us healthy.

Jesus, Son of God, you know the joys and challenges of the human body. Remind us that our bodies are temples to be cared for and honored. Help us to treasure all the details in the vastness of the human body, no matter its color, race, geography, education, health, income, or gender. Amen

October 17

God of Wholeness, heal all whom you will. For those who cannot be healed, cure their spirits so they may find peace and comfort in life and with those whom they hold dear. Surround all families of those who need medical care so that they can celebrate life and wonder.

Give us eyes that can see the invisible wounds of people's spirits—the unseen wounds that push people down.

Give us ears to hear the silent pleas for justice and fairness—the unspoken pleas that dishearten people when not addressed.

Give us hearts to unite with people whose own hearts are buried in years of neglect or abuse—abandoned hearts that are little and mean-spirited because they have shriveled up.

Give us stomachs to join with the hunger of people who are overlooked—the hunger of yearning for a life that is filled with love and meaning.

Give us the will to address the overwhelming need for medical care when there is no money—the fear of the unknown that paralyzes people.

We can do none of this without your strength and power. Amen

October 17

Reds, yellows, browns, and oranges. What beautiful colors you give us this time of year, O God. The variety in the seasons keeps us mindful of change in our lives and reminds us that change can be good and beautiful. The seasons also teach us that whatever is now will be different soon. Thank you for these beautiful reminders. Amen

October 18

Watchful and Caring God, sometimes a person's name just pops into my head. I may not have seen them in weeks or even years. For some reason I know that I need to hold them up to you but I don't know why. I trust that you know what they need. So my prayer for a person who comes to mind is, "Holy God, I don't know why this person came into my consciousness but you know what they need right now. I give them to your watch and care." Amen

October 19

Wondrous God, I have a question. Do you ever just want to scream? When we continue to do stupid stuff, do you just want to stomp us and smash us like a bug? Oh right, you like bugs. Well, then, I have another question. How do you tolerate our being so careless in the choices we make? Do you expect us to grow from our waywardness? Or maybe you hope we'll realize we're not as hot as we like to think we are? I honestly don't know how you do it...you know, loving us in the midst of all our mess that we created. Just please, keep on loving us anyway but show us how to grow in good ways. And please, help us offer that same kind of love to others. Amen

October 20

Wonderful Counselor, Frederick Douglass once said, "If there is no struggle, there is no progress. Those who profess to favor freedom, and yet deprecate agitation, are men who want crops without plowing up the ground. They want rain without thunder and lightning. They want the ocean without the awful roar of its many waters."

Holy God, give us courage to be about your business in the world. Give us wisdom to know what to do and when to do it. Give us resolve to continue following your lead even when we feel we are failing or walking in darkness. Strengthen us with your counsel by providing us companions along this journey of courage, wisdom, and resolve. Comfort us in the times of thunder and awful roar. We ask this of you, God of love, grace, judgment, and strength. Amen

—From

http://www.goodreads.com/quotes/6398-if-there-is-no-struggle-there-is-no-progress-those

web search 10.24.12

October 21

Maker of All Things, thank you for the rhythms of life. Mondays lead to Fridays, weekends lead to Mondays, waking leads to sleeping, crawling leads to running, life leads to death, and arriving leads to leaving. Thank you for never allowing the rhythms to stop no matter how much we might want it. Sometimes we do not want sleeping to give way to waking when the alarm clock goes off. Certainly we don't want to relinquish life and yet appreciate the gift of death when suffering is intense. We seduce ourselves into the idea that what life is today is what life will be always. Sometimes we yearn for that to be true and at other times, we hope that the situation of today will quickly be over.

Help us remember your wisdom as written in the biblical book of Ecclesiastes, "For everything there is a season, and a time for every matter under heaven." We trust you as guide of our lives. Amen

—From

Ecclesiastes 3:1

October 22

Wow, awesome, wonder of wonders, super amazing, stupendous, terrific, sweet. Holy God, all these terms apply to you and how we experience you at times in our lives. How come we rarely use them for you in our everyday lives? What holds us back from unashamedly proclaiming your love, grace, and power? Hum-m-m-m. Help me meditate on that one. Amen

October 23

God of This Day, be with me today.

In whatever location I find myself in, be with me.

In whatever conversation I join in, be with me.

In whatever creative time I experience, be with me.

In whatever frustrating challenge I face, be with me.

In whatever joyous time I celebrate, be with me.

In whatever impatient situation I find myself in, be with me.

Keep me mindful of your constant presence. Give me wisdom and guidance for every minute of this day. Help me reflect your grace in all my doings and beings today. Amen

October 24

Most Gracious God, thank you for this anniversary date for me. I was ordained to be a Minister of Word and Sacrament in the Presbyterian Church USA on this date in 1982. I had no idea about the journey you would lead me on as a minister. Thank you for being with me every step of the way, even when I was not sure where you were. You certainly led me in totally unexpected paths. The entire time I was in seminary, I thought I was preparing for small church pastorates but that was not in your plan. What a surprising God you are. And yet, the path you opened up for me was exactly the one that best fit my passions, strengths, areas of growth, and energy. You have truly blessed me. Let me never take that for granted. Amen

October 25

God of the Ages, thank you for wrinkles. I see my
ancestors in my face as more and more wrinkles
appear. I see my grandmother's eyes now when I look
in the mirror. I see my mother and her mother when I
look at my neck. I see other relatives as my body
continues to change. And when I look at the
generations who follow me, I see our family in their
faces, expressions, and movements as well. Thank
you for this continuity that becomes evident with each
wrinkle. Who knew? Only you could know the
wonder of this gift. Amen

October 26

Lover of All Children, kids are just so darn cute when they are little. We ooh and aah over them. At what age do we begin hating them? When do they stop being children whom we want to rescue, cuddle, nurture, and teach? When do they become *those people*? When do they become abusers, addicts, gang members, rapists, thieves, and all those people whom we label with negative words? What's wrong with us as human beings that we allow situations that create *those people* out of precious, darling small children?

Forgive us. Help us stop the wounding, the abandonment, the abusing, the ignoring, and the demeaning of children. Strengthen us to always see and embrace the precious and cherished child in every person whom we encounter—no matter their age or situation. Amen

October 27

Friend of the Poor, they keep coming: people who need help with rent or utilities, people who are hungry, people who are homeless or need a job or more education. We reach out to them with the help of many others in the community. But it's never enough and they keep coming. They keep coming. We hurt for them. We laugh with them. But they keep coming.

Keep our hearts soft for them. Inspire others to help us help them because they keep coming. We cannot do this work without your help and support because they keep coming. Please keep coming to us so we can be there with them. And then we'll realize that we're not there for them, they are here for us. Thank you. Amen

October 28

You have got to be kidding. You want us to what? You want us to love all those people who irritate us so much? I'm not talking about all those people out in the world that I know we're to reach out to. I'm talking about that person in the workplace who irritates the fool out of me or the family member who makes me feel judged all the time. I'm thinking of the person from the past who just won't remain in the past and keeps popping up at the most inopportune times. We're supposed to love them?

But I can't. Hard as I try, I just can't love them.

Oh, I get it. I can ask for you to surround them with your love, especially when I can't? I can hold them up for you to wrap them with your compassion? I can acknowledge that I'm not ready to fully embrace them? When I give them to you to hold close, then I'm beginning to find my way toward you and them?

Okay, help me do that...to pray for them to experience your love and compassion because I can't quite get there yet. Giving them to you to love is the first step for me to be loving and open-hearted to them. Thanks, I'll try—with your help. Amen

October 29

Holy God, I want to be rich. Someone once said that there are two ways to be rich. One is to acquire great wealth. The other is to acquire few needs. I want to be rich the second way. Poke and prod me to discern between need and want. Push me to release attraction to latest trends in decorating, clothing, and technology. Nudge me to relinquish much of the stuff in my house by giving it to friends, family, and secondary markets. I want to acquire new ways of thinking about material goods and old ways of conserving, making do, and thriving with fewer goods. Please, God, make me rich. Amen

October 30

God of All Good Gifts, thank you for volunteers who work because they love to and not because they have to or they get paid. They inspire us with their dedication and their love. They challenge us with their unique perspectives about life, programs, and issues. They move us with their commitment. They are truly saints among us.

Holy One, call forth ways for us to use our talents and passions whether we receive financial reward or not. Instill in us the love of using your gifts just for the pure joy and satisfaction of being with you. Amen

October 31

What do I call you today when ghosts, goblins, and witches abound? Some groups use this day to try to scare the hell, literally, out of people. How does that work for you? Some people dress up as people they would never think of being in real life. I guess it is okay to try on a different persona for a day. But scary stuff??? I think that today, Halloween, I prefer to call you God of love, God of grace, God of hope, and God of glory. I'll leave the spooky, scare-the-hell-out-of-you stuff to others. But on the other hand, one of your names is Holy Spirit. Maybe you like all this Halloween stuff! Me? I'll keep my porch light off and be the Halloween Scrooge. Amen

November 1

Lord God, today is All Saints Day. We remember all those people who have gone before us in death. And yet, Giver of Resurrection, they are still with us because of the gifts they gave during their lifetimes. Ann gave deep love and commitment to family. Diane gave passion and joy in serving others. Hank gave the triumph over a difficult past to become a blessing to others. Jimmy gave the delight of shared childhood games. Bill gave leadership and the willingness to change direction late in life. These and so many others are still in our hearts and minds. Thank you for the wonder of their lives now and forever. Amen

November 2

God of the Loving Heart, sometimes I simply don't feel very loving. I don't want to love that person who said those hurtful words. I resist reaching out to someone whose very presence I resent. Sometimes the only thing I can pray is *God, help me want to want to love that other one*. Is that enough for today? I pray to you that it is. Amen

November 3

God of Light and Sun, thank you for people who come into my life who challenge my usual ways of looking at the world. They push me to think in new ways and even though I may not agree, they deepen my relationship with you and them. Please, Jesus, keep them coming…just not too many at one time, okay? Amen

November 4

God of Comfort, you know that people are suffering because of impending loss of a loved one, a job, a home, or something else that is dear to them. Help us open our hearts to their pain so that we may offer what they need, in whatever small ways we can. Especially let us say words that acknowledge their hurt instead of offering cheery platitudes that discount their situation. And, O Lord, when we cannot or do not reach out to them, forgive our self-protection and motivate someone else to provide for them what we cannot. Amen

November 5

God of Strength, why did I have to learn that the interplay of dependency on my part helps keep poverty in our midst? I do not like being disturbed that way! I knew that sometime people felt entitled to whatever services were offered in the community. I acknowledged that I've met people who prefer to be dependent so that I and others will take care of them.

I do not want to admit to you and myself that sometimes I inadvertently encourage dependency when I say, "Here, let me do that for you" thereby implying that the person is indeed powerless. I like being someone who knows how to do things rather than teach someone how to accomplish the task. I like feeling powerful and important. I like being the giver. It makes me feel good.

Holy God, help me work myself out of a job by helping others to claim their own God-given gifts, strengths, and paths. Never allow me to help poverty continue by allowing people to be inappropriately dependent on me or on the services available in our community. Amen

November 6

Most Merciful God, you have taught me that ignorance continues poverty. Well, God, the stereotype of people who are poor is that they are ignorant. You and I both know that's not true. They may have different kinds of knowledge than I do. But ignorant? No. The knowledge they have and the knowledge I have just are very different sometimes.

Nevertheless, I confess that I am indeed ignorant. I truly do not understand what living in poverty feels like. I refuse to acknowledge how certain government policies keep people down when they are trying to pull themselves up. I don't want to know how my lifestyle, my purchases, or my demands for bargains continue to keep people in low paying jobs, in dead end options, and without hope. Put people in my path who will educate me and open my eyes, mind, and ears to the lessons I need to learn. Uphold me as I go through a conversion process about your beloved sons and daughters who often remain invisible to me. I depend on your grace and pardon. Amen

November 7

Fountain of Wisdom, thank you for people who, even though they live in poverty, have significant wisdom to share from their lives. Thank you for Betty who said, "I learned not to wallow in pity," and for Towanda who said, "I learned to have patience with myself and people in general. To accept the things I can't change. Not to complain about what I couldn't do but enjoy what I could do. Thank God for waking us to every day." These angels speak powerfully about your grace and love for us. We bless you for their words. Amen

November 8

Awesome God, open my eyes, my heart, and my ears so that I can catch a glimpse of the wonder you surround me with. Help me not take for granted the many, many blessings and instances of grace that nudge me each day. Alert me to opportunities to share the wonder of relationship with you. Without your loving care, life is colorless. Thank you for my life's richness. Amen

November 9

God of Joy and Celebration, this month for my particular family is birthday month. We honor birthdays of grandmothers, grandchildren, great-grandchildren, nieces, sons, and sisters-in-law. Thank you for the span of years these lives represent, the joys each has experienced, and the miracle of each one's contributions to the richness of our extended family. We are grateful for the gift of each other as we've faced the heartaches of life and the challenges of struggles. Be with each of us as we continue to explore the wonder of the lives you are creating for us.

Holy God, remind us of those whose families do not hold them in honor, who feel they are only a burden to their closest relatives, or who are just another mouth to feed. Help us to find ways to let others know they are treasured, if not by those whose blood they share, at least by those who are their sisters and brothers through your blessed Son. Amen

November 10

Source of Blessing, so many people rarely experience the joy of being blessed by you through a parent, a teacher, a co-worker, or a friend. They hurt because of that lack. They act in peculiar ways sometimes in trying to force a blessing. They feel worthless because they do not get noticed and loved in ways they seek.

Giver of All Good Gifts, open our hearts to those around us who yearn for someone to care in deep ways, to love them with abandon, or to embrace them with unreserved joy. Help us reach out and be your blessing. Amen

November 11

Okay God, sometimes I simply don't want to pray. I don't want to acknowledge that you are in my life. I just don't want to bother with caring, compassion, and truth. Justice is what other people are supposed to do. Not me. I need a vacation from you and your expectations of me. I need to rest without being hounded by your calling me. What do you say? Hey, what's your answer? Did you hear me? What happened to you? Where did you go? Where are you? I need and want you. Amen

November 12

Our Refuge and Strength, thank you for giving me feelings—even those I wish I didn't experience.

When I get frustrated, you are helping me learn more about patience.

When I grieve, you are teaching me to live in the present, not past or future.

When I am angry, you are teaching me acceptance of others and myself.

When I hate, you are teaching me humility that I am also what I hate in others.

When I am embarrassed, you are teaching me the joy of laughter in the unexpected.

When I am anxious, you are teaching me to relax into your love and grace.

Keep teaching me through the living of my days. Amen

November 13

God Our Father, on this date in 1973 I became a mother. Well, that's not exactly true. I gave birth to my first-born son all those years ago. Becoming a mother was and is an ongoing process. Each step along the way has brought new joys and challenges to motherhood. Learning to care for a newborn baby is vastly different from parenting a fully grown man who is himself a husband and father. Thank you for this wonderful gift.

Because of the deep satisfaction and richness I experience as a mother, I can only stand in awe and wonder at the love you have for each of us, your children. I am overwhelmed when I look back on our journey together so far. I bow in gratitude and thanksgiving for the amazing love you share with me and the opportunity you allow me to experience as a parent. Amen

November 14

Lord God, today I pray with the psalmist who laments: "Rise up, O Lord; O God, lift up your hand; do not forget the oppressed. Why do the wicked renounce God, and say in their hearts, 'You will not call us to account'? But you *do* see! Indeed you note trouble and grief, that you may take it into your hands; the helpless commit themselves to you; you have been the helper of the orphan. Break the arm of the wicked and evildoers; seek out their wickedness until you find none....O Lord, you will hear the desire of the meek; you will strengthen their heart, you will incline your ear to do justice for the orphan and the oppressed, so that those from earth may strike terror no more." Amen

—From
Psalm 10:12-15, 17-18

November 15

Keeper of Our Souls, keep my soul. When I am in meetings that challenge my patience, help me listen first before I speak. When I am incensed by another's ignorance of justice, help me take a deep breath and if possible, use the opportunity to educate the other person. When someone speaks from prejudice or stereotypes, help me connect with them to open new ways of thinking. And when I display signs of injustice, challenge another's patience, or speak from my own long-held misconceptions, give me a gracious teacher who can speak your truth to me in ways that I can hear. Amen

November 16

God of All Times and Places, what in the world do we do with all our grand ideas? We think we've come up with a plan to solve a major problem. Then as we move into our processes, we realize that we hadn't considered a particular scenario, the inadvertent consequences that our "solution" caused, or the longer-than-expected time frame.

Remind us that *you* are the one who brings about the kingdom of God and *you* are the impetus behind goodness. Keep us humble in our ambitions. Don't let us stop working for justice and mercy just because things did not go as we planned. Open our eyes for alternatives and for your guidance. Keep us motivated and yet aware that success lies only in your will. Amen

November 17

Source of All That We Have and Are, we praise you and magnify your name. We confess that sometimes we think our praise of you gets us what we want. We figure if we say the right words in the right way, then you will reward us with what we want. We even wonder what kind of God you are when you do not give us what we ask when we ask! We sometimes wonder if we want to worship such a seemingly fickle God.

Forgive us, Holy God, for suggesting that you bless people on merit. Forgive us for implying that material blessings are directly related to how much you, God, love us. Forgive us for shutting the door to your grace to ourselves and others by our false reasoning. Let us praise and glorify you, as the Apostle Paul says, in whatever state we find ourselves and not for what we expect to get but for what we've already experienced with you, Father, Son, and Holy Spirit. Amen

--From

Philippians 4:11

November 18

God of Creation, thank you for the quirky blue chairs I had in my office for decades. I inherited them when I moved into that office building. As trends changed, people either loved them or hated them. But they stayed with me as long as I stayed in that office. Those blue chairs provided a sanctuary for people who struggled with decisions, celebrated joys, wiped tears, or told silly stories. They embraced all who sat in them in ways beyond my imagining. Who knew that you had blue arms, O Most Loving God! Amen

November 19

God of Life and Health, help me to listen to:

The meaning of the silent spaces between the words;

The fear behind the anger;

The desire clouded in excuses;

The hurt encased in boasting;

The truth under the lies.

I know you listen to me. Help me to offer this same gift to others. Keep my interruptions and advice to a minimum so I can be fully present to the other. Make me aware of your voice in the midst of conversation. Guide my hearing into your ways. Amen

November 20

Searcher of Hearts, how in the world do you tolerate all you find in our hearts? You know that we can do really good things and receive many compliments for our efforts. But you also know that deep in our hearts, we have other, darker motivations for the good we do. We even convince ourselves that we are as great as others believe we are.

Thank you for loving us anyway. Keep guiding us in your ways. Continue to love us into the people you are creating us to be. Help our hearts be purer and more blameless. We desire to be your good disciples but we need your help. Amen

November 21

God of This Day, help me with my anger. I get angry over things big and small. I need help. I feel anger when:

Someone tries to make me do something I don't want to do.

The toilet paper roll is empty.

A person never listens to me…ever.

I get another idiotic e-mail and don't realize that it is dumb until I'm halfway through reading it.

Someone does not understand the word "no."

I misplace my keys.

Help me shake off these and other triggers. Convince me that these kinds of anger take me away from you and from living with my heart wide open. Give me ways to move away from the heat of the moment and to breathe in your spirit of peace. I cannot do this without you. I'm counting on you. Amen

November 22

God of History, I never see this date on the calendar without remembering the horror of learning that the President of the United States had been assassinated in Texas. Help us move beyond killing as a way to solve our problems or show our dissatisfaction with how the world is currently operating. Help us remember that one of your names is Prince of Peace and lead us to follow in your footsteps. Amen

November 23

O God, help me to be thankful. There is so much that I take for granted:

Water when I turn on the faucet in the bathroom;

Heat when I bump up the thermostat;

Light when I flip the wall switch;

Comfort when I slip into my bed;

Safety when I lock the front door at night.

Some of my brothers and sisters do not have these things. Help me to never use these gifts without deep gratitude. Make sure I constantly remember those who must live without water, heat, light, comfort, or security. Lead me to discover ways to ensure that everyone has these things I consider necessities. I depend on your strength and guidance, most loving Father, Son, and Holy Spirit. Amen

November 24

God of Our Fathers and Our Mothers, thank you for all those who have gone before us. They clear cut the paths we walk today. They invented, advocated, taught, challenged, struggled, meditated, and dreamed so that we can enjoy the fruits of their labors.

Help us to always consider how our actions, inventions, teachings, challenges, struggles, meditations, and dreams are laying the groundwork for those who follow us. Be with us so that the legacy we leave will be cherished and not regretted. Amen

November 25

God of Travelers: In the ancient scriptures, we learn that your people were travelers...from Ur, from Egypt, to the land of promise, from Israel, to exile, and back again. In all those travels, you were with the people. We ask today that you be with travelers as they go to celebrate holidays with friends and family. Even for those who experience hardships in their journey, whisper your love and grace so they will feel sustained.

We especially pray for those who have no one to celebrate with or who have nothing they can be thankful for. Make us so uncomfortable in our comfort that we search for ways to reach out to those who are lonely and battered by life. We need you to unsettle us. Amen

November 26

Searcher of Our Hearts, search me and know me and then help me know myself. Help me to see those things that I choose to keep hidden and to claim those good things that are also me. Lead me to the serenity of being the person you are creating me to be. Thank you for knowing me from my mother's womb. You are my love, my grace, my blessing, and my joy. Amen

November 27

Strong God of Truth, we lift up those who delight in twisting the truth for their own purposes. We pray for those who speak what they earnestly believe to be the truth but it is not your Truth. We beg you to hold in your grace those who seek the truth but do not find comfort in their search. We pray for all of us who have a bit of the truth. Help us come together so that together we may put our bits of truth together to come closer to the Truth to which you are calling us. Amen

November 28

I choose today to be special, Lord, and so I pray with the psalmist, "I will extol you, my God and King, and bless your name forever and ever. Every day will I bless you, and praise your name forever and ever! Great is the Lord, and greatly to be praised; his greatness is unsearchable....The Lord is gracious and merciful, slow to anger and abounding in steadfast love....The Lord lifts up all who are falling, and raises up all who are bowed down. The eyes of all look to you, and you give them their food in due season. You open your hand, satisfying the desire of every living thing. The Lord is just in all his ways, and kind in all his doings. The Lord is near to all who call on him, to all who call on him in truth. He fulfills the desire of all who fear him; he also hears their cry, and saves them. The Lord watches over all who love him....My mouth will speak the praise of the Lord." Amen

—*From*

Psalm 145:1-3, 8, 14-20a, 21a

November 29

Rock of My Life, how do I know that I'm building my life on rock and not on sand? How do I know that I'm following your will and not my own or what someone else is telling me? In what ways can I discern how to be a faithful person and not one who floats along without intentional commitment to you, Jesus, my Lord and Savior? How shall I live with grace and not grouchiness? With joy and not judgment? With commitment and not carelessness? How will I know? Who will guide me? Where do I seek? I search for your answers and guidance. But sometimes…sometimes…well, you know how I am. Please do not leave me alone. Amen

November 30

God of Hope, Light, Peace, and Love, we are on our journey to Bethlehem with this Advent church season. We are challenged to wait while the days get shorter and the Christmas "machine" gets cranked up into full force. Teach us the patience of waiting with eager anticipation for the coming of your new world, where suffering is no more, death has been conquered, and love abounds. We see the vision as though we're looking through smeared and dirty glass. And yet we wait for the clarity of your kingdom. Be with us while we wait. Amen

December 1

God of New Birth, Paulo Freire has said that former oppressors, "[c]onditioned by the experience of oppressing others, [see] any situation other than their former ...[as] oppression. Formerly, they could eat, dress, wear shoes, be educated, travel, and hear Beethoven; while millions did not eat, had no clothes or shoes, neither studied nor traveled much less listened to Beethoven. Any restriction on this way of life, in the name of the rights of the community, appears to the former oppressors as a profound violation of their individual rights—although they had no respect for the millions who suffered and died of hunger, pain, sorrow, and despair. For the oppressors, 'human beings' refers only to themselves; other people are 'things.'"

Holy God Who Chose To Become Human, break open our hearts to our oppressive ways. Help us change them, no matter how much we do not want to. Amen

—From

Paulo Freire, Pedagogy of the Oppressed, The Continuum Publishing Company: New York, NY, 1997, p 39

December 2

God of This Day, this morning was one of those mornings. You know what I mean. The dogs woke me up very early...before dawn!!! The freezer wasn't working properly. A kitchen utensil broke while I was preparing my breakfast. My inbox had boring messages and requests. It was just one of those mornings.

Remind me that you are with me today...no matter what. Reinforce for me that *those mornings* are gifts, too. They shake me up from my complacency. They require me to exercise patience. They challenge me to let go of the past so I can be present to the now. Thank you for the gift of this morning. I just don't want another one like any time soon. Okay? Amen

December 3

Proclaimer of Justice, please forgive our head shaking and clucking.

When we hear that more than 50,000 people live below the poverty line in our community, we shake our heads and cluck.

When we learn that a child dies of starvation in our world every five seconds, we shake our heads and cluck.

When we find out that about 1000 people are homeless here, we shake our heads and cluck.

When we see people dying in our world because of preventable diseases or war, we shake our heads and cluck.

Strengthen our resolve to do something about these conditions rather than simply shaking our heads and clucking. Don't let us relinquish our caring and responsibility for our sisters and brothers so easily. Amen

December 4

Emmanuel, Christmas Day is still weeks away and I'm already sick of Christmas music, store decorations, and commercials selling us more Christmas cheer. I want you to be with us. That's your name, Emmanuel, God-with-us. I want your peace, love, hope, and joy—not all this artificial stuff. Don't get me wrong...I love all the Christmas nostalgia and generous hearts of the season. It's that I don't want the fake stuff to replace you in my heart, my home, or my world.

Holy God, Emmanuel, keep me close because so much entices me away from you this season. Amen

December 5

Wait, wait, wait. That's all I seem to do. Wait for the phone call to be returned. Wait for answers for aligning calendars for holiday visits with family and friends. Wait for input about a project I'm working on. Wait for the water to get hot for my cup of tea. Wait, wait, wait.

Oh…that's what Advent is all about? Waiting? Waiting for Jesus, the Savior of the World to be born? Waiting for the good news of God's love to become human flesh? Waiting for insight into the wonder of the arrival of God-with-us, Emmanuel?

God of Advent, I need help with waiting…please. Amen

December 6

God of All Possibilities, help me to believe that.
Amen

December 7

Dearest Son of God, today I pray using some words of the Advent hymn:

"Come Thou long expected Jesus, Born to set Thy people free;

From our fears and sins release us; Let us find our rest in Thee....

By Thine own eternal Spirit Rule in all our hearts alone;

By Thine all-sufficient merit raise us to thy glorious throne." Amen

—From

Charles Wesley, "Come, Thou Long-Expected Jesus", The Presbyterian Hymnal, Westminster/John Knox Press: Louisville, KY, 1990, page 2

December 8

God of Comfort, one of the Advent scripture readings begins with the words, "Comfort, O comfort my people." We don't do a very good job of that, do we?

When people are crying, we look the other way.

When people are failing, we blame them.

When people are needy, we offer pittance.

When people are afraid, we say "Get over it."

Forgive us for not reaching out with comfort to others. We don't intend to be mean and uncaring. We just are. Push us to be comforters. Lead us to offer to others what you so generously give to us. Amen

—From

Isaiah 40:1

December 9

O King of Glory, an Advent hymn, "Lift Up Your Heads, Ye Mighty Gates," has these words:

> "Redeemer, come!
>
> I open wide my heart to Thee;
>
> Here, Lord, abide.
>
> Let me Thy inner presence feel;
>
> Thy grace and love in me reveal."

This is my prayer. Amen

—From

Georg Weissel, trans.Catherine Winkworth, "Lift Up Your Heads, Ye Mighty Gates", The Presbyterian Hymnal, Westminster/John Knox Press: Louisville, KY, 1990, page 8

December 10

"O Come, Desire of Nations,

Bind all peoples in one heart and mind;

Bid envy, strife, and discord cease.

Fill the whole world with heaven's peace."

O come, O come, Emmanuel. Open our hearts to your peace. Bind our wills to your grace. Fill us with your ways. This we pray. Amen

—From

Latin c. 12th century, trans. Henry Sloane Coffin, "O Come, O Come, Emmanuel", The Presbyterian Hymnal, Westminster/John Knox Press: Louisville, KY, 1990, page 9

December 11

God of This Advent Season, you promised us that

"The desert shall rejoice and blossom as a rose

For the ears of the deaf shall hear and the blind, their eyes be opened.

For the tongue of the mute shall sing and the lame will dance with gladness.

As the ground will become a pool and the dry land springs of water."

We hold tight to your promise. Keep us steadfast in our hope and give us signs of your work in us and in our world. Amen

—From

Gracia Grindal, "The Desert Shall Rejoice", The Presbyterian Hymnal, Westminster/John Knox Press: Louisville, KY, 1990, page 18

December 12

God of Wonder, all around us lights twinkle, carols play, and sweets delight our tongues. But for some, this time of year is torture. They remember happier times, their aloneness is magnified, and their poverty of resources or spirit is monumental. Every holiday sentiment is like a nail in their flesh, crucifying them in their desolation. They wander in the desert when others gather in clusters to celebrate. They grieve while others hug loved ones. Keep us mindful of these, your hurting children. If we are to give solace, open their hearts to us. If we are to hold them in prayer while others give tangible signs of your love, remind us to remember. If they are to be isolated from human intervention, come to them as angels or stars or in any other way that they can feel your presence and know your love. Make us the prayers we offer. Amen

December 13

Who am I to dare to come to you in prayer? Do you really mean it... that you really, really love me...better than the person who loves me most in the world? Can that be real? Is it true? Is that what you are trying to tell me yet one more time during this Advent season...that you are coming to be with me, human-me, in-the-flesh-me? You are coming to show me yet again the wondrous love you have for me and everyone else? This is more than I can fathom. I want to believe. Help me. Amen

December 14

God Who Overcomes Death, Life, Angels, Rulers, Things Present, Things to Come, Powers, Heights, Depths, and Everything Else in All Creation, does anyone really care? Do people wonder about you? Do people strive to serve and honor you? Does any of it really matter to anyone? Do people really believe that you are you?

Sometimes we need a sign. Is there a possibility that you can provide that assurance for us? Amen

—From
Romans 8:38

December 15

God of Light, the long nights reflect the dark of our souls. The world outside is barren with nature gone dormant. Even with the twinkling lights of the holiday season, gloom surrounds us. Our faith holds on...barely. The despair of the night feeds into the day. Time crawls with the dark.

Creation yearns for your light to renew us once again. We beg for your presence among us. We crave your tangible evidence of peace and hope. We hunger for your joy that is greater than our understanding. We await your coming. Please hurry. Amen

December 16

Holy God, thank you for ruts. Otherwise, we would not know how good we feel when we get out of one! We get stuck and don't even realize how we've limited our scope or our expectations. We are comfortable in our ruts. And then something happens. You perhaps? We get pushed out of our complacency. After a bit, that feels wonderful. Thank you for placing us in situations and places where we have to grow. Thanks for not allowing us to stagnate. Make sure you stay right with us in this new way of thinking and living! Amen

December 17

O Lord Most Holy, we come into your presence with thanksgiving, singing your praises, and proclaiming your goodness and grace. We come to honor you and to glorify you.

We say the right words. When we're honest with you and ourselves, we acknowledge that sometimes the words we say sound hollow to us. We really don't mean them. We just know that we're supposed to say them if we're *really* praying. We want to deeply mean them. We want to feel them. Open our spirits and our hearts so that the words we say to you become the most important words we ever utter...to anyone! Amen

December 18

God of Joy and Peace, help us become peacemakers. Let us not be content to be peace keepers...those who keep things smooth rather than deal with the undercurrents that bubble below the surface.

Give us courage to name the things that hinder peace or continue conflict.

Give us wisdom to know how to be peacemakers so that we do not add to the unrest.

Give us knowledge to claim your definitions of truth rather than our own.

Give us calm to be centers of insight even in the midst of disturbances.

We claim your peace as we hear your counsel to "be not afraid." Amen

December 19

God of All Good Gifts, sometimes we do not appreciate the gifts you give us because we compare them with what others have. I want to be able to dance and move like Beyoncé. That's not going to happen. But I can get up and move and shake and dance as only I can. Thank you for the gift of my style of dance.

I want to be able to paint like Andrew Wyeth. I can't. But I can pick up a brush and smear colors on the paper. I can even take art classes if I want to improve my skills, but let's face it, I'll never be a Wyeth.

I want to be svelte and limber like Olympian athletes but no way! And yet, I can get out and walk as if I'm a champion…and I am…in my own way.

Thank you for my many gifts. Support me as I learn to appreciate them as the perfect gifts for me. They're mine and they are stupendous! Thanks, God. Amen

December 20

Our Source and Our End, you consistently amaze me with the many ways that you come to me. I'm seeking solace and choose a book off the shelf that speaks to my soul in ways that only you can do it. I need to connect with a soul friend and that person calls me for lunch. I'm wrestling with a solution to a problem and the television show gives me the clue that unlocks my dilemma. I need a push to move from my "pity party" and someone I respect looks me in the eye and pushes. I need to learn and you send the teacher.

Thank you for the myriad ways you let me know you are in me, around me, beside me, in front of me, behind me, and under me. You are my source and will be my end, now and forever. Amen

December 21

Our Refuge and Strength, today we begin our final walk toward Bethlehem and the miracle of your coming into our world as one of us. That is beyond our comprehension. We know both the joys and struggles of being human. That you would take this on overwhelms us with love. Help us to honor this gift through the lives we lead. Especially this week let us not be overcome with false trappings of the season but let us reside in your peace and grace. Help us never to take for granted this gift of yourself that we are about to celebrate. Amen

December 22

Most Wondrous God, fill me with

> Peace...not anxiety;
> Joy...not cattiness;
> Love...not judgment;
> Compassion...not hurry;
> Hope...not resignation;
> Faith...not abandonment.

Let me be for others as you are to me. Amen

December 23

Holy God of Christmas, I want to revel in the joy of being with family and friends this holiday season. I don't want to remember those who have no family or friends with whom to celebrate. I want to enjoy presents given with love and thoughtfulness. I don't want to have to think about people for whom Christmas is just another day to get through. I want to eat all the special foods of our family tradition. I don't want to have to think about people who are hungry or who eat whatever they can find in the dumpster. I want to live in a rosy, loving world, full of happiness and wondrous happenings. I don't want to have to accept that for others the world is a bitter place, full of hardship, terror, and suffering.

You know me. You know that for a time I'd like some blinders on my eyes. I trust that you love me even when I need my eyes to be filled for a brief time with only sparkles and lovely swirls of color. Thank you for the beauty you surround me with. I am grateful that you are not allowing me to believe that this bubble is all there is. Fill me with the miracle of Christmas so that once again I will yearn to be with and care for those who are lonely, hungry, and suffering. Amen

December 24

O Holy Baby,

Tonight you have no home of your own, and you are born.

Tonight your parents are simple folks and you come to them, needing them for life itself.

Tonight you are born in simplicity whereas churches celebrate with ornate buildings and fixtures.

Tonight you bring abundance to our world and we see only scarcity.

Tonight you seek only love and we offer everything else.

Come to us and open our hearts to welcome you as you want to be welcomed. Amen

December 25

"Joy to the world! the Lord is come:
 Let earth receive her King;
Let every heart prepare Him room,
And heaven and nature sing…
No more let sins and sorrows grow,
Nor thorns infest the ground;
He comes to make His blessings flow
 Far as the curse is found….
He rules the world with truth and grace,
And makes the nations prove
The glories of His righteousness,
And wonders of His love…."
Thanks be you to you, O God. Amen

—From

Isaac Watts, "Joy to the World," The Presbyterian Hymnal, Westminster/John Knox Press: Louisville, KY, 1990, page 40

December 26

God of Earth and Air, Height and Depth, the celebration has come and gone. Presents are unwrapped, food eaten, and some people are even taking down their decorations. We are eager to get back to business as usual. No more of this joy and good cheer.

Most Wondrous God, keep reminding us today and every day of the height and depth of your love for each of us. Be graceful with us when we forget the miracle we have just honored. Push us to connect with those babies who have grown up into people we ignore, dislike, or attack. Help us to keep the spirit of love, joy, and peace in our hearts and lives. Amen

December 27

God of All Generations, we must not forget the love that we have just celebrated because you chose to become one of us humans. And because it is your love that we remember, we can:

Reach out to those who hurt.

Laugh with those who find delight in this world.

Sing with those who celebrate.

Mourn with those who grieve.

Dance with those who find enjoyment in living.

Cry with those who can do nothing else.

Sit with those who need companionship.

Allow us to be with you in caring, laughing, singing, mourning, dancing, crying, and sitting. Only with you in our lives, can we be the people we want to be for those before us, behind us, and beside us. Amen

December 28

"The people I know who have made any radical shift in the way they live have had some exposure to poverty on a consistent basis. When the crossing is made from the world of the elite to that vast world of the poor, they cease to see their work as sacrificial. They begin to care about different things, to acquire a whole new set of values. They are doing what they most want to do."

God of Love, as this year draws to a close, give me the heart for shifts that more closely align with your will. Amen

—*From*

Elizabeth O'Connor, The New Community, Harper and Row: New York, 1976, p 22

December 29

"Remember the first time God turned the world upside down? He did it with a small band of disciples and almost no resources except the power of God. We dare not underestimate what God can do with our small loaves and fishes if we give ourselves without reservation to his world changing conspiracy."

God of the Smallest Details, loosen my fear so I can give myself without reservation to your ways of loving and living. Amen

—*From*

Tom Sine, The Mustard Seed Conspiracy, Word Books: Waco, TX, 1981, p 236

December 30

"We cannot subsidize the poor into silence. Nor can we evangelize into isolated soulful bliss those we have deemed unfit to be our neighbors. The poverty we now face in the inner city is deeper than merely the lack of material possessions. It is a poverty of the spirit created and reinforced by persistent rejection. It is what Mother Teresa identifies as the deepest poverty of all— to be unwanted."

Spirit of Life, break open my heart so I can reach out to others: friend, family, neighbor, acquaintance, co-worker, nameless one on the street, and distant foreigner. Help me find tangible ways to assure people that each and every one of us is wanted through your vast love and mercy.

Let my words be heartfelt...not empty.

Let my actions be true... not fruitless.

Let my will be merciful...not uncaring.

Let me be as you lead me to be. Amen

—From

Robert D. Lupton, Return Flight -- Community Development Through Reneighboring Our Cities, FCS Urban Ministries, Atlanta, GA, 1993, 1997, pp 45-46

December 31

"To live.... threatened with resurrection."

God of the Past, Present, and Future, to you a day is like a thousand years. But to me, this day marks the end of the year. This is a time of remembrance, reflection, and resolutions. So now, I commit to you my one resolution: to live threatened with resurrection. May I continue in this New Year to reflect what the resurrection means to me, how it changes and chastens my life, and the ways it impacts my relationship with you and others. With gratitude and humility I pray. Amen

—From

Julia Esquivel of Guatemala

http://www.livingjustly.org/2012/04/10/threatened-with-resurrection/ web search 10.24.12

Refrigerator Prayers for Ordinary People

What ordinary people are saying:

"These are 'real' prayers…questions and concerns written in words that could easily come into my head. This is a book I would give to a lot of friends along with a lint roller! (see September 10)." Pat F.

"Templeton's prayers … speak to the struggles all humans experience. The prayers are reverent, yet intimate, and will give readers a blessing to begin each day with." Carolyn L.

"Templeton has chosen topics that everybody has prayed about but she uses such thoughtful language that we all can identify with the questions and answers to God. Each of us has wanted answers…Templeton's approach is so comforting." Betsy H.

"Wonderful. *Refrigerator Prayers* give me a sense of direction to pray for others instead of only myself when rushing through life's hurdles." Naomi C.

"From illuminating the topic of poverty to highlighting the hustle and bustle of everyday living, these prayers are tools for the ordinary person to ask God for perspective and guidance." Kate C.

"Templeton weaves our personal love for God with our everyday encounters, encouraging us to reflect on the details of our lives and be ever thankful." Emily W.

About the Author

Beth Lindsay Templeton, Founder and CEO of Our Eyes Were Opened, Inc. is a public speaker, Presbyterian Church U.S.A. minister, and writer. For almost thirty years, she worked at United Ministries, a non-profit in Greenville, South Carolina, where she worked with both "the have-nots" and "the haves." Since 2012, she has focused on a ministry with "the haves" so they can enlarge their understanding about people who live in poverty in order to decrease judgment and increase compassion.

Beth works with congregations, schools, universities, medical facilities, civic groups, and businesses in Greenville, SC, and around the country. She is the author of: Loving Our Neighbor: A Thoughtful Approach to Helping People in Poverty, Understanding Poverty in the Classroom: Changing Perceptions for Student Success, Conversations on the Porch: Ancient Voices-Contemporary Wisdom, A Coat Named Mr. Spot, More Conversations on the Porch, and Angelika's Journal. She is the poverty expert in a 5-part DVD series titled Servant or Sucker.

Beth is a graduate of Presbyterian College and Erskine Theological Seminary. She and her husband have three married sons and four grandchildren.

44170748R00222

Made in the USA
San Bernardino, CA
09 January 2017